girlSource

a book BY and FOR young women

ABOUT relationships, rights, futures, bodies, minds, AND souls

Created by the GirlSource Editorial Team

Jessica Barnes, Wanda Chan, Shirley Escobar, Ilene Franco, Ingrid Garcia, Aisha Ivory, Faye Liang, Diane Martinez, Lina Shatara, and Diana Valdivia

Launched by the GirlSource Book Publicity Team

Ashley Bizzell, Peaches Bizzell, Sharon Lo, Krystal Maxwell, Blanca Suarez, and Angel Thackaray

Carried on by all the participants of GirlSource—past, present, and future

TEN SPEED PRESS
Berkeley/Toronto

A girlSource Production

Ashley Bizzell

Yo, I be the one and only too fly to be lonely Ashley. I was raised in Riverside, California, and now reside in the Yea Area. I attend Gateway High School and I am the junior class president. I love my sister, singing, writing, dancing, and those who care.

Peaches Bizzell

Hi, my name is Peaches Bizzell. I'm 16 years old and I am a sophomore in high school. I am a beautiful princess from heaven above, born and raised in Riverside, Southern California. I have four brothers and two sisters. I'm the second youngest. I come from a big family and I'm loved everywhere I go.

Sharon Lo

My name is Sharon and I'm 16 years old. I am a Chinese-American born and raised in San Francisco. I come from a hard-working family that came to America for a better lifestyle. My future looks bright from where I'm standing. In my free time I'm out and about with my friends, or losing myself in a good book on rainy afternoons.

Krystal Maxwell

Hey there, I'm Krystal. My last name is Maxwell and I'm 17. I live in San Francisco, California. I started working at GirlSource in 2001 when I joined their Technology and Leadership Program and then became a Teaching Assistant. Life's been pretty much the same ever since.

Blanca Suarez

Hey everyone, my name is Blanca Suarez, but most people know me as Baby. I am 17 years old, a step away from becoming an adult. I attend an all-girl Catholic high school in the city where there's always something crackin', San Francisco, where I was born and raised.

Angel ThacKaray

Hi, my name is Angel. I'm 14 and I'm in the ninth grade. I recently participated in my first GirlSource program and am currently finishing another. After graduating high school, I plan to attend a college somewhere on the East Coast. Then I want to go to medical school so that I can become a pediatrician or maternity ward nurse. Those are my main goals in life!

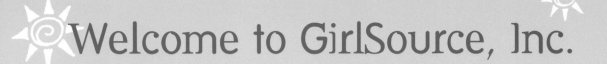

Welcome to GirlSource, Inc.

GirlSource empowers young women by giving them meaningful work that teaches life, leadership, and media skills in the process of creating useful products for other young women. For us, Girlsource is much more than a job; it's a place where we can be ourselves and speak our minds without being judged, and where we are encouraged to use our own experiences and creativity in everything we do. We build our self-confidence and self-image by helping other young women. The skills we've learned and experiences we've had at Girlsource have shaped who we are today, and who we will become in the future.

How did this book happen?

Soon after GirlSource was founded, the staff designed and distributed a survey to over 500 young women in the Bay Area to find out which issues in their lives concerned them most. Smaller groups of young women then met to hone the survey responses down to specific topics of interest. They identified their top issues as sex and relationships, managing stress, dealing with violence and discrimination, getting a job, and staying healthy. In 2000, GirlSource interviewed and hired ten young women from diverse backgrounds and communities to create a real book inspired by these topics. Within nine months, the GirlSource Editorial Team became editors, researchers, writers, teachers, speakers, photographers, interviewers, art directors, and advocates for their own issues. They created and self-published the first edition of this book to great reviews under the title, *It's About Time!*

Since *It's About Time!* was originally published, GirlSource has continued to hire young women to create products by and for young women, many of them inspired by this book. Through our Technology and Leadership Program we built (and continue to feed) a young women's health and well-being website, called **www.GirlHealth.org**. Participants in our Community Leadership Program create young women's resource and referral guides. Our Young Women's Speaker's Bureau (of which the GirlSource Book Publicity Team is a part) trains participants to speak out about the issues that face young women today.

As the next generation of Girlsource, we join the GirlSource Editorial Team and all Girlsource participants—past, present, and future—in welcoming you to our world. Please visit us at **www.GirlSource.org** to find out more about us and all the work that we do!

Write to us!
book@girlsource.org

Jessica Barnes

I'm a 16-year-old African-American young woman living in the Visitation Valley area. I am the second oldest child of six, and I plan to be the first in my family to go to college and graduate. I want to achieve a career in medicine, as well as be a role model for my younger siblings and prove to myself that I can do all the things that I put my mind to.

Wanda Chan

I'm a 16-year-old Chinese-American born and raised in San Francisco. I speak Cantonese and English fluently. As a full-time student I want to major in psychology and minor in English or history. Some of my hobbies are drawing Japanese Anime and reading. Astrology and numerology fascinate me.

Shirley Escobar

I'm a 17-year-old Latina, born and raised in San Francisco. For the past three years I've been involved in working with different communities, as well as participating as an advocate for my peers. I felt that it was important for me to help create this book because it was a way to share my experiences with a lot of other young women.

Ilene Franco

I'm a 16-year-old hyper and crazy Latina, born in Los Angeles and raised in San Leandro. This was my first real job, and I wanted to help other young women out there with crucial life topics, as well as with learning to make positive choices. I hope you like our book!

Ingrid Garcia

I was born in Guatemala and grew up in the Mission District of San Francisco. At 18 years old, I love all forms of art, including photography, silk-screening, painting, writing, and acting. I am also a LocoBloco dancer (an Afro-Brazilian drumming/dancing group). There are different paths to take in life, and if you choose the wrong one, it's okay, because you'll be stronger and learn from it.

Aisha Ivory
I'm a 19-year-old African-American, born and raised in the Fillmore District in San Francisco. I've come a long way from the projects and violence. Along with graduating from high school and continuing my education in medical assisting, my most important goal is to raise my eight-month-old daughter, Taeja, to be a proud, independent young woman without any insecurity and enough motivation to take her wherever she wants to go.

Faye Liang
I was born in China and I've been here in San Francisco for almost two years. I am a full-time high school student. My dream is to be a diplomat in the future, and I hope I can learn all kinds of different languages in the world!

Diane Martinez
I'm a 15-year-old Mexican born in San Francisco, where I'm now in high school. I read and speak English and Spanish. My co-workers and I are trying to give you options in life instead of advice. The choice is yours and no one can do for you what you can't do for yourself. I hope our words can help you!

Lina Shatara
I'm an 18-year-old Palestinian-American young woman. There are many strong women in my life, including my mom, grand-mother, aunts, and two sisters. I have a passion for art and pho-tography. I enjoyed drawing illustrations for this book. I would like to use my talents in the future to help my community in a positive way.

Diana Valdivia
I'm a young woman athlete. I was born in Mexico and raised in San Francisco. I play on softball, tennis, and basketball teams at my high school. My plans for the future are to graduate from college and become an architect or a child psychiatrist. For now, I'm looking forward to graduating from high school. I had a lot of fun making this book with my colleagues.

Table of Contents

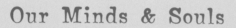

Our Minds & Souls

Our Bodies

Our Relationships

Our Rights

Our Futures

Introduction

We created this book in order to give young women empowering options instead of advice.

Our mission was to gain knowledge and confidence through others' and our own experiences in order to teach young women to survive, to take pride, and to love themselves from the inside out. We wanted to get our voices out and to help young women.

In the process, we shared our life experiences, wrote our stories, took photos and were photographed (a lot!), led workshops, brainstormed our visions (over and over again), networked with other

organizations, attended conferences, met famous women, overcame our fears, commuted all over San Francisco, made friends, learned about ourselves, had fun, and expressed our opinions (about everything!).

As strong and intelligent young women we've come this far with our life experiences. We want you to know and learn about yourselves and to feel like you can make your own choices. It's about time young women had a resource created by other young women.

This book is for you!

–The GirlSource Editorial Team

Ilene Frano

Shirley M. Escobar

Diana Valdivia

Lina Shatara

Faye Liang

Wanda Chan

Aisha Ivory

Jessica Lynn Barr

Ingrid Garcias

Diane Martinez Vega

How do i know if i'm stressed out?

Stress is a part of life, no lie, but it isn't always bad. It can motivate you to study more or try harder at sports. Stress is the body's reaction to any event or situation that is threatening, disruptive, or challenging.

Being "stressed out," on the other hand, can be harmful physically, mentally, and emotionally. It's easy to feel overwhelmed by the demands on your life. Doing well in school, taking care of your siblings or child, pleasing your boyfriend or girlfriend, showing up to work on time, getting along with your friends or parents, or simply trying to be "normal," rational, and mature—can all cause stress. Too much stress can make you feel anxious and depressed.

Sometimes you can get rid of the thing that's stressing you out—you take the test, or do the work. Sometimes you can't—maybe it's family problems or an illness—then you just have to figure out how to stay sane for yourself.

Things That Can Stress You Out

☆ Moving to a new home or school

☆ Parents separating or getting divorced

☆ Your family worrying about money or jobs

☆ Getting bad grades

☆ Not being invited to a party or dance

☆ Trying out for a play or a sports team

☆ Making decisions about sex or relationships

☆ Helping friends in trouble

☆ Writing a huge term paper

☆ Taking care of your baby or brothers and sisters

☆ Figuring out your sexuality

☆ Fights happening at home

☆ Parents checking up on you

☆ An abusive boyfriend or girlfriend

☆ A violent neighborhood

☆ Having an illness or medical condition

☆ The death of a loved one or friend

☆ The constant irritations of daily life

"I feel stress when I have too many responsibilities at school, work, and home. I might have tests and papers due, or at home I might have to clean the house and my younger sisters won't help with the mess. When I get really stressed out, I just don't do anything; I watch TV and sleep a lot. Sometimes talking about it with my mom helps. Usually she is comforting and listens to what I have to say."

Lina, 18

"The last time I got stressed out was when Social Security sent me a letter saying I was going to get cut off two days after my last day at work. I kept saying to myself, 'How am I gonna make it? How am I gonna make it?' I mean, I have to take care of my daughter and I have to pay rent. My mother, she's really trying to get me for being in her world, and so she makes me pay rent. So I went down to the unemployment office and showed them the paper that showed I was cut off, so at least I felt a little better. But not that much better because I don't want to be sitting on welfare. That's not me. I don't want the government to be taking care of me or my child."

Aisha, 19

How can i deal with stress?

At Home

If your parents nag you, remind them that you're growing up. Call up a relative you love but can't ever make time for and spend some time hanging out. If problems at home make it difficult to be there, find some other safe places. Try the school library, a friend's house, or an after-school sports program.

At School

Sit down and figure out exactly what your priorities are. Put your energy into a few things and say no to other extracurricular activities.

Make a list of everything you have to do and then cross out each thing you accomplish. Save the list and look at it at the end of the day. Easy does it, but do it. Pat yourself on the back.

Talk to a guidance counselor about your worries. She may be able to refer you to a support group or a peer counselor. Sometimes just getting it off your chest feels good.

Try to find a quiet place to study. At home, unplug the phone and turn off the TV. If it's still too noisy, find a place like a café or library where you won't be bothered.

With Your Friends

Cut back on the time you kick it with friends who pressure you too much.

Set boundaries with people who irritate you by limiting their phone calls or steering clear of them.

If you're in an abusive relationship, take steps to get out of it (see page 53).

"I remember that when I first attended ISA High School, I felt hell'a lonely because all my good friends were in different high schools. So I was very afraid to go to school and afraid to talk with people. Every day, I just went to school by myself and was very quiet in class and never tried my best to do anything. I remember one very ugly thing happened to me in PE class. Some boys played on me. They danced sexually and talked nasty to me. They laughed at me and asked me to be their girlfriend. I dropped the PE class. However, I still felt very lonely and scared at school. So I started to cut classes. For almost a month I couldn't find a way to help myself out. Finally, I made up my mind to go back to school again. This time, more classmates were nice to me and I finally had some friends."

Littlefly, 18

Signs of Being Stressed Out

○ Worrying all the time

○ Crying or blowing up a lot

○ Getting headaches, stomachaches, or backaches

○ Breaking out in rashes or hives unrelated to allergies

○ Feeling tired all the time

○ Having constant constipation or gas

○ Eating too much or not at all

○ Being unfocused and on edge

○ Biting your nails, grinding your teeth, picking at your skin, or cutting or burning your body

Ways to Fight Stress

☆ Talk to someone whom you can feel calm with.

☆ Get more sleep by going to bed earlier or taking naps.

☆ Take an hour to do whatever makes you feel warm and calm: listen to music, take a long bath, go for a run, read a book, see a movie, or go to the park by yourself.

☆ Figure out how to let your anger and frustration out safely—punch your pillow.

☆ Find ways to laugh—call your funniest friend, turn on your favorite sitcom, or read the comics.

☆ Find a dog or a cat to play with.

☆ Find exercise you like. Kickboxing is good if you've got some frustration to burn off. Dancing and running will make you feel relaxed too.

☆ Drink at least two to four more glasses of water than you do now.

☆ Cut back on all those caffeinated soft drinks; the boost they give is only temporary and you'll feel even worse when you crash.

☆ Eat at least two more pieces of fruits and servings of veggies than you do now.

☆ If you smoke, quit. You'll need all the clean air you can get if you're stressing.

☆ Make time to slow down: Start by releasing your shoulders, dropping your jaw, flexing your feet, wiggling your toes, and breathing deeply (see page 21 for meditation techniques).

☆ Yoga not only helps with strength and flexibility, but also is extremely relaxing.

How can i feel better about myself?

Self-esteem comes from inside—it's how you see yourself. No one can give it to you. Having good self-esteem doesn't mean you're happy all the time, but you know your own worth, and you know that you're okay just as you are.

Having a strong sense of yourself means understanding how you fit into the world around you. The following "senses" contribute to high self-esteem:

A sense of security. This is so basic, but so real. When you feel safe at home, at school, in your neighborhood, and on the job, it's easier to feel good about yourself. We're talking physical safety and emotional safety here. It's good to be free from constant putdowns.

A sense of belonging. Your family plays a big part in this one, too. If you feel connected to others and accepted by them—whether they're family, friends, or classmates—it's easier to keep your head up.

A sense of competence. There's something you do well, and you know it. For some young women, it's drawing. For others, it's geometry, cooking, dancing, basketball, or writing. Whatever it is, doing it makes you feel confident, in control, and ready to take on new things.

A sense of who you are. If you've got this, you're not easily swayed or confused by peer pressure. Of course, this trait is tricky, because you're still deciding who you are. But it's important to know what you value and what your limits are, and accept responsibility for the things that you do.

A sense of purpose. Having this means you have your own goals and the will power to see them through. You don't have to nail down the Meaning of Life before you're 20, but you do need to know what makes you happy and fills you with passion. You know what general direction you want to head in.

The Esteem Team

In this culture, there are lots of messages about who you should be as a young woman, and it's easy to wind up with low self-esteem. Sometimes friends, family, and community knowingly or unknowingly contribute to our poor self-image. Sometimes the media contributes to the problem, too, by making you feel like you'll never live up to some impossible ideal. Though sometimes you may feel helpless when you hear these messages, you can fight back.

Family and Friends

The situation: Family and friends can be judgmental, even if they say they are making a joke or just trying to help you. They don't always realize that what they say hurts your feelings. If they cap on you a lot, you might even start to believe the things they say.

The solution: Be strong and take a stand by telling the person who is hurting you how he is making you feel. Whether or not he stops, you've made your feelings clear, and that's the first step to fighting back. If he continues to make negative comments, you can warn him that you will stay away from him until he respects your wishes. This is hard to do, so get some support from your close friends while you build up the courage.

Peers

The situation: Peers, especially in high school, do a lot of teasing and name-calling. Sometimes bullies do it because they've been teased themselves. Still it sucks. Looks, race, religion, gender, sexual preference, and ambitions are all things that bullies may tease you about. Whatever happens, don't believe what the bullies are saying—they're just looking for your vulnerabilities.

The solution: The most important thing is to stick up for yourself. Show bullies that you won't put up with obnoxious teasing by telling them to stay away. Sometimes, you just have to put them in their places once to make them stop. However, if they don't, try to remove yourself from that situation. Ask the teacher to assign you to a different seat, avoid that particular hangout, or talk to a counselor about the problem.

"Check it out, when I got my report card last semester, my dad said to me, 'You didn't get at least an A-minus in English. What are you stupid or just lazy? You need to study more.' So I told him, 'I did study and I tried my hardest and I'm proud of myself and I think you should be too.'"
Sandy, 16

"I used to define myself as other people saw me. In high school, you have to fit in. But now I create my own image and I have more control. I see myself in a bigger light."
Angel, 19

> "I swear, the next time one of those girls in the hallway tells me, 'You need to lose weight, girl, I can see your stomach hanging out,' I'm gonna tell her, 'I don't have a problem with my body, so why should you?'"
>
> Seoufa, 17

The Media

The situation: Our society judges a woman by her appearance, so we often find ourselves trying to fit into society's standard of beauty. When you look at television, movies, music videos, beauty magazines, and advertisements most of what you see is the same type of woman. You see thin, sexy, white, clear-skinned, "flawless" young women.

No wonder some of us feel bad about ourselves. We are constantly being told by the media that if we don't fit into that standard of beauty, we are not attractive. This portrayal is quite the opposite of all the real and wonderful women in the world.

The media also feed you the idea that you need to change yourself to fit society's ideal. Look through many women's magazines; there are always advertisements about ways to lose weight or a product that will make your skin flawless. There are pills, surgeries, and weight loss programs all telling you to change. The beauty industry makes a lot of money by convincing women that they are not okay as they are naturally. They want us to think we need their "miracle" products to transform ourselves. They want us to spend lots of money on their products. With all these messages, it's easy to doubt the beauty of your body.

The solution: You only have one life to live, so why waste it worrying about how fat your thighs are or how to achieve that perfect complexion? There is more to life than thinner thighs. The most important thing is to start loving yourself from the inside out. This means not putting your looks down at any time. Never forget that you are intelligent, creative, talented, and loving—wonderful all around.

Stay away from media that depicts women as objects in need of fixing. Seek out media that depicts women in a realistic manner (see the box to the right).

Also write to companies and magazines that show young women in an unrealistic or unattainable light. If people all start to fight back, we might see some changes.

TIPS

Practice Liking Yourself

* Do something nice for yourself every day.

* Find things that make you feel good about yourself that don't involve buying some product. Maybe it's doing a friend's hair, running, taking a walk, or playing the guitar in a band.

* Volunteer with a community group.

* Write down five things that you like about yourself.

* Surround yourself with people who are supportive.

* When you look at yourself in the mirror, practice being kind to yourself. Tell yourself what about you looks great and strong. Keep those negative voices out of your head.

Check Out Alternative Media

Magazines

Bitch magazine: A feminist response to pop culture, devoted to insightful commentary on our media-driven world.

Moxie: Produced and written for 20-something women who want more out of a magazine than fashion, beauty, and tips on how to get a man. This magazine encourages young women to define themselves from the inside out.

Books

Where the Girls Are: Growing Up Female with the Mass Media by Susan J. Douglas

The Body Project: An Intimate History of American Girls by Joan Jacobs Brumberg

Wake Up, I'm Fat! by Camryn Manheim

Websites

Adios Barbie (www.adiosbarbie.com): A body image site for every body. This website talks about women's issues and offers ways to love your body.

Girls Figure In! (www.sfnow.org): This site educates the public about the media's portrayals of women and the impact these representations have on young men and women.

How do i know what my sexuality is?

What does it mean if you begin to have feelings for someone of the same sex? Are your feelings sexual, emotional, or both? Being attracted to another girl or woman doesn't necessarily mean you are a lesbian, any more than being attracted to members of the opposite sex means you are straight.

You don't have to define your orientation right now—or even ten years from now. It's your option to experiment and take all the time you need to understand your sexuality.

The important thing is that you get comfortable with who you are.

> "I get a lot of questions like, 'When did you first come out?' and 'How did you know you were a bi-dyke?' That disappoints me about people sometimes because it's like, well, when did you figure out you were straight? Why does it have to be some big revelation? I could date [my discovery] back to when I was in first grade when I liked this girl and thought she was my special friend, but it's not like I was saying, 'Hi, I'm gay' or 'I'm bi' in first grade. Who ever does that? For me, it was not a big decision, it was just something I let myself say out loud and I wasn't going to hide my sexuality."
>
> Rochelle, 20

TIPS

Coming Out

* Come out first to somebody you feel very comfortable with and who already accepts you for who you are.

* Make sure you have a social safety net, a friend or group of friends who can understand what you're going through when you come out. Many towns have a support group or hotline for gay, bi, or transgendered youth.

* Choose a time when the person you are telling is in a reasonably good mood and is not already distracted by some major event going on in her own life.

> "Heterosexism: the belief in the inherent superiority of one pattern of loving and thereby its right to dominance.
>
> Homophobia: the fear of feelings of love for members of one's own sex and therefore the hatred of those feelings in others."
>
> from *Sister Outsider* by Audre Lorde

How do i come out?

You can have sexual feelings and experiences with other girls and women, and still not identify yourself as gay. But you may still feel that you need to tell your friends and family about your sexuality. The process of coming out is different for each person. It's important to listen to your heart, not what the media, your parents, or even your friends might be telling you to do. And whether it is easy or difficult for you depends on who your family and friends are and whether they are willing to accept you. Their feelings towards your sexual orientation may change over time too.

Definitions

Bisexual or bi: A person who is sexually attracted to both men and women.

Gay: A man or boy who is mainly sexually attracted to other men or boys. This word can also describe any individual who is sexually attracted to people of the same gender. The words "gays," "gay people," or "gay community" are often used to refer to gay, lesbian, bisexual, and transgender individuals.

Lesbian: A woman or girl who is mainly sexually attracted to other women or girls.

Queer: A broad term that includes anyone breaking "the rules" about sexuality and gender, usually used as a self-identifying and empowering term by individuals within this group.

Transgender: A broad term for anyone who is breaking "the rules" about sexuality and gender, people who don't identify with either gender—or who identify with both—or people who are born with ambiguous genitals and were surgically altered at birth to become one gender.

Transsexual: People who feel out of synch with their own gender and choose to identify with and live as the other gender. Transsexuals often feel "trapped" in the wrong body. Some take hormone therapy or have a sex-change operation to change their gender.

Transvestite: A person who dresses up like the opposite sex, including crossdressers (who dress realistically like the other sex), drag queens and kings (who dress flamboyantly like the other sex).

Interview with a Bisexual Young Woman, 19

Q: How did you know you were bisexual?
A: In middle school I started to like girls, but I didn't really show it. I think before that time we had so much schoolwork that I didn't really pay attention to the fact that I liked girls. After I came here from Taiwan, I started to like girls. I have strong feelings for girls, even though I'm bi.

Q: How old were you when you first realized your feelings?
A: 15 years old.

Q: Did you tell your family you are bisexual?
A: My relatives here searched my diary and they found out, but they didn't believe it.

Q: Why didn't they believe it?
A: They thought I probably felt lonely here. They were scared and they couldn't find any reason why I would like a girl.

Q: Why didn't you tell your parents?
A: I tried to tell them before, but I think they didn't believe it. My parents are unable to understand that I am gay, so they wouldn't believe me anyway. So I just choose not to tell. They are still traditional, so I don't think they would accept it.

Q: How did you think they would react if you told them?
A: I think they would be mad and sad and they would think because I came here [to the USA], I changed. They would think that being here influenced me.

Q: Did you tell your friends you are bisexual?
A: It is too much pressure for me to hide anything, so I chose to tell my close friends.

Q: Who did you tell and what did you say?
A: One girl, but mostly guys. I just said, "If I were bi, what would you think?"

Q: How did they react when you told them?
A: At first I was scared, but I think they were pretty understanding and they accepted.

Q: How did you feel after you told them?
A: I feel I finally have someone I could talk to, that I could face some problems with.

Q: Did you feel relieved?
A: Not really, because the ones I really wanted to tell are my parents and my family. I think I still hide lots of things in my life. It feels hard to have to lie.

"I remember starting to think being gay was wrong in middle school. The meanest teacher in the whole school was a gym teacher and a lesbian, so it was easy for everybody to say bad things about her and about being gay. I started saying pretty early that I can't be gay. I was hiding a lot of stuff and was really an angry kid, so I started smoking pot and eating acid and Ecstasy... Later, I met my first girlfriend the summer after I graduated high school and I came out and it was just such a release of tension and stress, like 100 pounds got lifted. I didn't have to pretend any more. I was like, OK, this is who I am."

Rachel, 23

"First I had to come out to myself and just lift off layers of denial, then I had to come out to my parents. When I first told my mom, she asked me if this was just a phase and I told her no. It's still kinda hard for her. I actually had the first good conversation with her about this just two weeks ago."

Anonymous

"I was explaining to my mother why I didn't want to stay in New Jersey when I came back East with my girlfriend because there was a lot of homophobia and discrimination there. And she didn't seem to believe me wholeheartedly, she seemed to think the homophobia was just in my head. So I got really upset, but we hadn't really talked for years and I hadn't actually ever told her what my experiences were so I realized that maybe if I told her she would understand more. So I told her what I had been through and we had like a breakthrough. I told her it was more gay-friendly in New York and in the Bay Area. I mean out here I get looks everywhere I go but at the same time some of the looks are good."

Rachel, 23

How do i deal with depression?

Some young women describe their depression as feeling empty or numb. For others, the experience of feeling low is mild, and they wouldn't describe themselves as "depressed." And some people who seem energetic on the outside are actually depressed inside. The fact is, teenage girls are more prone to depression than boys, and by adulthood, depression is twice as common in women as in men.

Sometimes the everyday pressures of life just get you down. Other times, the causes can be very specific—low self-esteem, strained family relationships, deciding to have a baby, dealing with an abortion, struggling with schoolwork, a break-up with a partner or friend, the divorce or separation of your parents, or the death of someone you loved.

Some depression doesn't have to do with outside causes. Fluctuating hormones or a genetic tendency towards depression can make you feel depressed. And, if you live in a family with people who are depressed, you may feel the effects of their depression, while not being depressed yourself.

It's pretty normal to feel blue or moody some of the time. You might feel bad because of a hectic social scene or family problems that are out of your control. Some teens feel angry and powerless over bigger issues too: war, hunger, racism, sexism, homophobia, or environmental destruction. This kind of depression usually passes after a day or two.

If you notice that you have been feeling low or depressed for more than a few weeks, you may be experiencing depression that's more serious than just feeling blue or moody. In that case, talk to a counselor—serious depression is not easy to shake alone. There are support groups, counseling techniques, and also depression-fighting drugs that may help you feel normal again. You really don't have to feel lousy all by yourself.

Signs of Mild Depression

The signs of depression can be very similar to the signs of being overly stressed. Here's what to look for:

○ Mood swings

○ Inability to concentrate or make up your mind

○ Eating too much or too little

○ Sleeping too much or too little

○ General sluggishness

○ Low self-esteem

○ Feelings of emptiness, sadness, worthlessness, or simply not caring

○ Not wanting to get out of bed, or being a couch potato week after week

○ Withdrawal from social life, family life, or any school activities you used to enjoy

> "My depression started when my dad died. Nobody in my family answered my questions about why he wasn't around anymore. I didn't even know people died. Most of my family ignored me. Later on I was doing really bad at school. I was failing math. Then my mom had a new boyfriend who was an abusive drug addict who loved to put me down. I couldn't really sleep anymore. I felt very lonely and so empty inside. Sometimes I would cry all night and sleep all day. I started to do a lot of drugs. But no matter how much drugs I did or what kind, I always ended up more depressed. Until one day I went out with a guy and we just started to have a deep conversation about life. I told him what I was going through. He taught me that failing a class was not the end of the world. He told me that everything happens for a reason and that I'm a survivor and the problems that I had to go through only made me wiser and stronger. He was right but it took me a while to figure that out."
>
> Isabel, 18

Signs of Serious Depression

- You've been feeling depressed, sad, or irritable for more than a few weeks.
- You are feeling worthless, excessively shameful or guilty about things you have or haven't done.
- You have a difficult time concentrating or making up your mind.
- You are sleeping too much or too little.
- You are eating too much or too little.
- You have severe mood swings.
- You feel tired all the time and have no energy.
- You feel that nothing can make you happy—even activities that you used to love.
- You find yourself thinking about suicide.

If any of these statements describe you, talk to a counselor or adult whom you trust. Let's face it, you feel lousy. Braving it out might not get you anywhere, but talking to a counselor, a nurse, or one of your parents might. You don't have to feel this way. Help exists. Take it.

> "Anytime you're depressed, it's gonna take you a period of time to turn around. What I used to do in middle school a long time ago was I would keep like a depression diary or whatever, and every time I was depressed or mad I would write down what made me mad and why I was mad and then sometimes I would feel better. Then on a bored day, I would go back and read it, and I would be like 'Daa-ang, I was mad at that?! That was kinda stupid.'
>
> But the best thing you can do is keep yourself occupied. Go out with a friend, a friend that's gonna make you smile, make you happy. Or do something, take a walk, anything that's not gonna let you just dwell on the problem."
>
> Aisha, 19

What Can I Do About Feeling Blue?

Get some exercise. Studies have found that exercise really lessens depression. An active workout helps you release frustration and tension and causes your body to release feel-good hormones. So grab your bike and go riding through the park. Run or race-walk on a trail. Borrow an exercise video from the library and use it. Try a yoga class—some studios offer the first session free.

Pour your soul out on paper or in a journal. If you're mad at someone, write about how you feel in a letter that you never send. Sad? Write about the last time you were happy and see if you can make that moment come alive. Hurt? Write about why you feel that way and what would help you feel better. (Later you can come back to it and see if it was fair and sensible.) Try to identify the feelings you're having one by one. Or try this exercise: Fill in the rest of a paragraph that begins "People think I am ____. But in my heart, I know I'm _____."

Get creative. If painting, doodling, or drawing is your thing, pick up a paintbrush or marker and paint your feelings. Pick up your musical instrument and play or just sing.

Go outdoors. Go walking in the park during daylight; bring a favorite magazine if you like. The sunshine and indulgence in a good read will help nourish your soul.

Talk to someone who lets you be yourself without judgment or expectations. This can be a favorite relative, a friend, or a school counselor or peer counselor. While you're feeling blue, avoid the people who only make you feel worse.

Pump up the music. Lock your door and put on some music that inspires you, brings you joy, or makes you wanna dance. Keep the broken-hearted ballads at the bottom of the stacks for now.

Punch out a pillow. Long and hard, if you must.

Keep up with your grooming and hygiene. Looking as bad as you feel won't help matters, so at least take care of the basics—skin, hair, teeth, you know the deal. Looking better may jump-start your mood.

Try other activities. These can be unusual things that remind you that you're part of a larger community or are just plain fun. For instance, help out someone you like, pitch in at a soup kitchen, go driving through a nice part of town, read a fantastic book or story, sing in a choir—or in the privacy of your own room.

What do i do if a friend is suicidal?

When it comes to life and death, we're talking hardcore issues. It's not like most of us have had experience with suicide, so it's not easy to figure out what to do when someone you love is suicidal. It's easy to get caught up in her feelings and confusion.

When someone is suicidal, she's in a lot of pain and is crying out for help. Don't ignore the situation and hope it will go away. Learn the signs that someone is thinking about taking her life.

How can i tell if a friend is suicidal?

- ✔ She talks about suicide methods or about how people will feel when she's dead.
- ✔ She's withdrawing or losing interest in hanging out or going out.
- ✔ She says things that show she feels worthless or hopeless.
- ✔ She's attempted suicide before.
- ✔ She talks about death, wanting to die, or wanting to be "out of the way."
- ✔ She's behaving aggressively or destructively, like fighting, carrying or using a weapon, or breaking the law.
- ✔ She's unusually moody or anxious, maybe crying a lot.
- ✔ She's drinking alcohol or taking drugs excessively.
- ✔ She's giving away belongings or making other "final" arrangements that say goodbye.

What can i do to help?

The most important thing we can do to help a friend who is suicidal is to help her make it through that period when she has given up hope. Here are some strategies on how to help.

Talk to a responsible adult about your friend by yourself, right away—even if she reassures you she won't commit suicide.

Offer to go with her to get help. Whether it's standing by as she talks to a teacher, sitting around with her waiting for a peer or adult school counselor, or going to a family member, try to be there to see this through. Try not to leave her alone now.

Be a good, nonjudgmental listener. Say things like "I hear you," "I feel you," not "Well, that's not worth dying for."

Be supportive. Remind her of all the wonderful things she has done. Remind her that she is not alone, that you and others are there for her. Tell her that the bad times will go away, and that nothing stays this awful forever.

Be real. Tell your friend how upset you feel when she talks of suicide. Tell her how much she means to you.

If a Friend Commits Suicide

Losing a friend to suicide can be devastating. Often friends feel that they are to blame, or that they could have done something to stop the suicide. If a friend has committed suicide, you need to remind yourself that it is not your fault. Yes, grieve for that person and get help or support to help you. But remember that you can go on with your life without losing that special place in your heart for your friend.

How to Deal with a Suicidal Friend

Tips from Dave Paisley, San Francisco Suicide Prevention

☆ Try to set up a network of people she trusts who can call or check up on her on a regular basis. If you can, share the responsibility of keeping an eye on her.

☆ Don't make promises you shouldn't keep—especially about secrecy. You can promise to not broadcast your friend's troubles to peers, but you can't afford to keep something this serious a secret from adults who can help.

☆ Don't tiptoe around the "S" word. If your friend is always talking about feeling down or bad, ask if she's entertaining thoughts of suicide.

☆ Don't sidestep the "D" word either. In many circles, it's not cool to feel depressed. But if you can tell that's where your friend is at, listen up, lend her a good ear.

Who to Call: The suicide hotline is 1-800-SUICIDE. Also, try a hospital, health care provider, family member, teacher, clergy, or peer counselor. As a last resort call 911 if you have to.

How do i deal with death?

Ways to Help You Heal

Share memories of the deceased. Organize a poetry slam or a special youth-oriented memorial. Build a shrine for your friend for the Mexican Day of the Dead. Just gathering a few friends at somebody's home to tell jokes, look at photos, and share memories can help you all feel better.

Give yourself some time off from normal activities. Allow yourself to think about the person who died; think about the good, strong qualities that she had that you'd like to carry on in yourself. Write a letter or a poem to her in your journal.

Tell your parents or a close adult how you're feeling so that they don't expect you to behave normally for a while (sometimes a long while).

Take care of your health. It's tempting to punish yourself when you see and feel so much suffering after a death, but don't. Try to keep your regular diet, exercise, and sleeping habits.

Do something nice for a fellow mourner. Cook brownies, buy a take-out meal, offer her a ride, help her complete a chore, or rent a video and watch it together.

Talk to someone who won't shrink from your intense feelings. Try an adult family friend, a church parishioner, an empathetic teacher, or a guidance counselor.

Cut people some slack. It's not unusual for adults or young people to say foolish or insensitive things at a time like this. Forget it. People make such comments because they are uncomfortable with death, not because they're inherently mean or don't really care.

> "When my friend Adam died in a car accident, I didn't go to his funeral because I felt that I should remember him the way he is to me. I didn't want to see someone in the coffin that didn't resemble my friend. Later, I kept trying to keep myself busy so that I didn't have to think about what had happened. But one day I just snapped and woke up. I figured that I should deal with it and get out my feelings that I had bottled up for so long. I thought a lot about Adam and how he was one of the most intelligent, charming, and funny guys I knew. Now that I have had time to heal, I feel that he had a fulfilling life, even though it was short. He loved life and lived it to the fullest."
>
> Annette, 17

The Grief Cycle

This is a cycle folks go through over and over in the healing process. You may not go through it in this order, or you may revisit the same feelings over and over again for a long time.

Denial: Feeling numb or pretending the death didn't happen.

Anger: Asking questions like "What kind of messed-up God would let this happen?" or raging about how unfair the death is.

Depression: Feeling so overwhelmed by sadness that you can't imagine ever feeling happy again.

Isolation: You feel as though the death has made you much different from other people. You feel as though you are in a bubble of pain and you can't reach out. You may stay in your room or refuse to go out with friends.

Guilt: Wishing you had been nicer to the deceased earlier or feeling bad about still being able to enjoy life.

Acceptance: Resuming normal life activities, remembering the loved one fondly and sadly but accepting that she is really gone.

FACTS

* Suicide is the third leading cause of death for young people age 15 to 24. So much for the myth that youth live a carefree life.

* Females attempt suicide more often than males, but males complete their suicides more often. (According to Suicide Prevention Action Network USA, the male to female suicide ratio for the year 2000 was 4:1.) This may be because guys tend to use more lethal methods when they attempt suicide—shooting, hanging, or carbon monoxide poisoning., whereas girls tend to take pill overdoses or slit their wrists—methods that fail more often.

What role can spirituality play in my life

MIND/SOUL

Spirituality can play as big—or small—a part in your life as you want. In this society, it's pretty easy to let your spiritual side shrivel up and die sometimes. It can be hard for a young woman to relate to the religion put out by the church her parents made her go to. Or sometimes a young woman thinks it's uncool to rely on nonmaterial things like faith.

Cultivating your spiritual side allows you to fine tune a part of you that goes beyond your body and mind, allowing you to understand, feel, "see," and "know" things on a whole other level. Developing a spiritual self can help you feel more connected to other human beings, to nature, and to all living things. It can help you form a new generation of folks who want to stop destroying the earth—and each other. On the personal side, it can help a young woman find her place in the world.

There are many ways to lead a spiritual life, just like there are many ways to worship God or practice religion (although some organized religions will tell you there is only One Way). Organized religion offers us fellowship, structure, guidelines, and rituals designed to lead people to a more spiritual life, and ultimately, lead people to God or the Infinite. Some young adults were raised with this kind of structure in their lives and have grown to appreciate it as they get older. Others haven't been raised with it (or don't appreciate it), and yet want and need to nurture their spirituality.

Try experimenting with other religions and seeing which ones appeal to you. If you'd rather stay away from organized religion, try reading scriptures and spiritual texts. Create a "sacred things only" table in your room with family photos, beautiful twigs, leaves or stones, candles, chimes, and other things that are sacred to you. Below you'll also find some guides for prayer and meditation.

What Religion Does for Me

An interview with a young woman, 17

Q: What is your religion?
A: I belong to the Holy Spirit Association for the Unification of World Christianity. I think my religion helps me have better relationships with people and helps me be more open-minded.

Q: Have you always liked your religion?
A: Not always, because sometimes it's hard being around other people of different religions or who are not religious at all. Sometimes I feel not normal.

Q: Do you think it's important today for teens to be religious or spiritual?
A: I do because it gives them a greater purpose in life. It lets them be peaceful inside and out.

Q: How do you think teens' lives would improve if they were religious?
A: They would have great self-respect and respect for others. Violence would decrease too.

Q: What is a valuable lesson your religion has taught you?
A: Respect and love everybody no matter what they do, no matter what their faults.

"I don't believe in religions because a lot of people have had to die for their God. I also don't like how the Bible goes on about gay people. Gay people were created just like everybody else.

I'm sure there is a superior power, but you can't really say it's a He or She or It, because you don't have proof. I would have to see proof. I'm always willing to be open-minded to new ideas, and as long as I am open, then it's all right."

Wanda, 16

Ways to Pray

Give thanks. Showing appreciation—for food, for family, for love, for friendship, for talent, for shelter, or for all the "stuff" you do have—sharpens your awareness of the treasures all around you. Practicing gratitude sweetens your relationships with others.

Offer praise. This includes noticing out loud what's special around you, as in honoring an unusual moment, an awesome performance, a breathtaking view, or a funny interaction.

Ask forgiveness. If you did somebody wrong, apologize. But also spend some time with your own conscience afterward. As you pray for forgiveness, ask for the strength or wisdom to avoid repeating your mistakes.

"I think that people create their own heaven and hell and their own demons. I think we have free will and I believe that love is the greatest lesson of all and that everyone has to learn that. I kinda learned this on my own because my parents never took us to church because they had to go when they were young. They let us figure things out on our own and I'm very grateful for that."

Anonymous

What is meditation?

Meditation is a way of communing with your highest self—or the Divine within, depending on how you look at it. During prayer, people talk quietly or out loud, but in meditation, everyone listens. While meditating, you ask nothing and give nothing but your attention. Watch your thoughts go by without judging them. Focus on your breath, or on a single word or mantra until your mind is completely still. For teenagers living in a busy city, sharing a small home with family, this may be the hardest thing you'll ever do.

What good is meditation? Life is full of confusion and noise, but meditation is a way to quiet down. It's a way of toning and training your mind and spirit in the same way that running or weight lifting is a way of toning and training your body. Many people report that meditating regularly makes them feel more clear-headed, confident, and balanced, more patient, less moody, and more open to recognizing what is special and experiencing joy.

Ways to Meditate

Pick a time of day when your household is usually quiet. Is there ever a half-hour when nobody is home? Mornings may be better than late at night because your mind is usually calmer after you've had a good night's sleep.

Set aside 20 minutes to half an hour. Turn off the phone and close the door; this will help shut out distractions.

Sit in a straight-back chair or on the floor. You'll want to be comfortable, but erect and alert, not slouching and ready to doze off.

Try counting your breath: mentally say "one" as you breath out, then "two" when you breath out again, and so on, up to four. Then start over again at number one. If you get distracted or bored, train your mind back to counting your breath.

Pick a mantra or word to repeat. In several Eastern traditions, the word "Om" or "Aum" is considered the most sacred of sounds and when you say it slowly, you can feel the vibrations from your throat right on down to your belly. "Love" and "peace" are other good mantras. If you feel too silly or self-conscious to say the mantra out loud, hum it, or think it to yourself. Let it echo in your heart. Feel it. Be it.

One way to end your session is to imagine powerful beams of white light, or loving, healing energy, radiating out of you, above, below, sideways, all around you. Keep visualizing this light until it forms a huge protective balloon of energy the size of several city blocks. This will help you glow with positive energy as you go on with the rest of your day.

"When I go to church and see that it's all marble floors and gold, it's not very spiritual. I don't believe in [going to] church because they're all into politics and making money. Besides, when my family had the hardest time, our church didn't help us, they turned their backs on us. So I find spirituality in other places, like the earth. And I do believe in God."

Lina, 18

"Prayer is good for everyone, even if you don't have religion because it relieves stress and it helps you get in touch with yourself and with whatever it is that you believe in."

Anonymous woman

How do i stay in shape?

Y̶ou'll be much more likely to exercise on a regular basis if you're doing something you really enjoy. It doesn't matter if you walk, swim, dance, play court sports, or try martial arts like judo, tae kwon do, or capoeira. Just get your body moving.

Motivation

Pair up with a friend who also wants to get into shape and exercise together. Or join a team. If you like to exercise by yourself, try wearing a Walkman or Discman and using music or books on tape to keep from getting bored and to stay motivated.

TIPS

Why Exercise?

- have fun
- feel healthy
- stay in shape
- be strong
- get in a good mood
- get energized
- feel accomplished
- learn to defend yourself
- make friends
- gain discipline
- prevent illness
- sleep deeply
- feel high

Sports Are My Game

by Diana, 15

My heart was pounding and I could hear the rush of the crowd cheering. It was the last five minutes of our basketball championship and we were hustling—sweating and dehydrated. It was intense. I got hold of the ball and heard my teammates shouting, "Shoot! Shoot! Shoot!" When the team's working together, it's a great feeling.

For me, sports are fantastic. I got into sports when I was little, through my dad and my brother. They'd take me out to the park on sunny days, and I learned to pitch and throw the ball. When I grew up, there started to be girls' teams at school.

Now I play all kinds of sports—at the rec center, at school, in the fields. I like basketball because you're always running and it's competitive. Volleyball is a good team sport. You have to communicate at all times. I'm the best at softball, though, because I've played it the most. Tennis is great, too, because you have to concentrate so hard. I also like to work out. At home, my sister and I dance to techno, rap, and hip-hop.

Before the game, I try to eat less so I don't get cramps. I also eat more carbohydrates than usual because it gives me extra energy. I get really hungry after a game, and then I go home and eat really good food. After I play sports I can breathe more easily. I feel energized.

How do i start an exercise routine?

Why do you want to get into shape—to feel better? look buff? get healthy? Write down the specific goals you want to achieve like "I want to learn a new sport" or "I want to be able to lift 15-pound weights for two sets." Make a commitment to yourself that you're going to work toward these goals. This is something you're working on for you so you need to really believe and be committed.

You might want to reward yourself as you begin to achieve mini goals on the way to your larger goals. Think of little things you can reward yourself with to keep yourself motivated. You might also want to think of a larger reward when you achieve the big goal, though achieving that goal is a reward in itself!

The biggest benefits from exercise don't come immediately. But after you've been exercising regularly you'll feel your energy and self-confidence increase. You may start feeling like you can't do without it.

Tips from a Pro

by Pam, a professional personal trainer

Do what you like—especially at first. You're more likely to stay motivated if you're having fun. If you can't stand running, don't do it. Try to get to the pool twice a week instead. If you know you won't be able to get yourself into the water in the middle of winter, plan to dance or skate or play basketball or work out at the gym.

Set goals for yourself like "I want to learn to swim," or "I want to join a sports team," or "I want to start playing soccer even though I don't know how," or "I want to be able to run three miles."

Start slowly and build up. Trying to do everything all at once is a recipe for failure. Instead of running five miles the first time you hit the track, you could just go out and walk quickly around the block once or twice. Then you can build up to a more heavy-duty workout over time.

Schedule your regular, weekly routine for a time that's realistic. If you tend to want to go out with friends in the afternoon, then try exercising early in the morning. If Wednesdays are long days at school, then plan to exercise on Tuesdays and Thursdays.

Keep your commitment to yourself. If you plan to exercise every Tuesday, Thursday, and Saturday morning, put it on your calendar and consider it an important appointment that you have to keep. Treat your exercise appointment the same way as if you were meeting someone after school or showing up on time for your job.

Women Athletes in the News

While the American public is generally more interested in male teams, we're starting to hear more and more about women athletes in the news. Mia Hamm, Briana Scurry, and Brandi Chastain led the U.S. Women's Soccer Team to victory in the World Cup in 1999. Chamique Holdsclaw and Lisa Leslie are both WNBA Basketball All-Stars, and Leslie is also an Olympic gold medalist. Venus and Serena Williams, sisters, are tennis superstars, with trophies from Wimbledon, the U.S. Open, and Australian and French Open tournaments.

TIPS

* Even things like pushing a stroller and walking up stairs instead of taking an elevator or escalator can be good exercise.

* You can do sports on your own, with friends, or in the community. Free sports programs at local recreation centers often offer exercise classes and team athletics for girls.

* Find a mentor—a young woman or adult—who's into sports. She can encourage and guide you, as you become more athletic.

What's a healthy diet for me?

Food is fuel. It's what you need to create new cells for your skin, hair, nails, bones, muscles, and blood. Your body will feel best when you have enough calories, vitamins, and minerals, and a mix of carbohydrates, protein, and fat every day. If the balance is a bit off—either too much of one thing or too little of another—you may feel tired, headachy, irritable, or lightheaded.

The number of calories you need each day is based on your size, activity level, and your metabolism—how fast your body burns calories. You may need to take in 2,500 calories or only 1,500.

Though the number of calories you need may vary, people all need the same nutrients. Carbohydrates like grains and cereals, bread, pasta, rice, fruits, and vegetables are the basics of a diet—these give you energy to burn. Proteins like cheese, milk and yogurt, meat, fish, and beans provide amino acids for building body proteins, helping to fight infections, and keeping your body systems running smoothly. Fats in oils, nuts, and meats provide concentrated sources of energy and insulation and protection for important organs and body structures. You also need vitamins and minerals, found in varying amounts in most foods.

There are a lot of healthy ways to eat. You can find healthy foods from many different cultures that are not part of the "typical" American diet. In parts of Asia, for example, people eat a diet mainly of rice, vegetables, and fish. Central Americans eat lots of beans, corn, tomatoes, and chili. These foods have plenty of vitamins and protein. The way foods are prepared makes a big difference in how healthy they are.

Read the Label

The package may say "all natural" or "healthy" but still contain large amounts of fats or sugars. The small print on the back of the package—the information on the food label—is what counts. By law, packaged foods have to have their ingredients listed on the wrapper in the order of the amount used in preparation. So, there's the most of the first ingredient in the list and the least of the last.

Safe, Healthy Food

Many fruits and vegetables are sprayed with pesticides—chemicals that kill insects in the fields. The problem is that large amounts of pesticides are believed to cause allergies, break down our immune systems, and perhaps even cause cancer in our bodies. This has happened to farm workers who spend their time picking the crops.

Here are a few things you and your family can do to protect yourselves against pesticides:

At Home: Keep a scrub brush by the sink. Wash your produce thoroughly with warm water. Peel vegetables and fruits when you can.

At the Market: Shop at a local farmers market or buy farmer-direct and organic produce from the supermarket. Fruits and vegetables are fresher when they're trucked in directly from small farms. Pesticide-free (organic) fruits and vegetables are distinguished by state certification marks on the labels. When you buy at a farmers market or farmer-direct, you can discover cool new produce like star fruit or purple potatoes and peppers.

For more information on pesticides, see the PAN (Pesticide Action Network) website: http://www.pan-international.org/

Choosing Foods

Meats
Fish and chicken are healthier choices than red meat.

Eat small amounts of the meats that have a lot of fat in them like salami, pork, and bologna.

Vegetables
Fresh and raw are best.

Frozen vegetables are the next and then canned.

Fats
Broiling, baking, and stir-frying foods keep your fat intake low.

Eat deep-fried foods in moderation.

"Fast is last."
FAST FOOD in general has a very high FAT content but little nutritional value. Try not to eat fast food every day. If you're only near a fast food restaurant at lunch or dinner, pick healthier choices from their menu like chicken instead of burgers, and broiled foods rather than fried. Drink milk or juice instead of soda.

Water flushes out the toxins built up in your body and keeps you hydrated, so drink the recommended eight glasses of water a day or as much as you can.

> **"** My parents are immigrants. They grew up poor. For them to be able to buy meat and sweets whenever they want to means they've really made it. **"**
>
> Yamina, 16

You can tell a lot from the food label. The label says the amount of sugars, fats, and salt, as well as the percentage of the U.S. Recommended Daily Allowances (RDAs) of vitamins and minerals in each serving. Beware of the various kinds of sugars and fats that are used in packaged foods. Corn syrup, sucrose, fructose, brown sugar, maltose, and dextrose are all different forms of sugar. Shortening, lard, hydrogenated fat, coconut oil, palm oil, and canola oil are all different types of fat.

Learn to Cook

The cheapest way to get good food is to cook it yourself. If you don't know anything about cooking, ask your parents, grandparents, friends, or parents of friends. Or it could be cool to take a cooking class as a group with some friends who are interested in learning, too. The library's cookbook section also has a variety of recipes to check out.

Healthy Cooking

- Cook with less oil. When you do use oil, canola and safflower oils are the healthiest.
- Add herbs and spices rather than extra salt.
- Broil or bake instead of frying.
- Steam your vegetables.
- If you fry, use just a teaspoon of oil and then add water for more moisture. Avoid deep-frying whenever you can.
- Eat more poultry and fish, and less red meat.
- Use skim milk instead of whole milk, which has more fat.
- Eat colorful meals. If your plate has a lot of colors—green, red, yellow, purple, orange, and brown—it's more likely to have fresh foods and all the vitamins and minerals you need. Meals made of pale or white foods are generally not as nutritious as colorful ones.

Grow Your Own

If you have a backyard or balcony area that gets sunlight, you can grow produce in pots or planter boxes. Vegetables like tomatoes, baby lettuce, and chili peppers, and herbs like oregano and chives are easy to grow. Some neighborhoods also offer free garden plots to people who want to grow vegetables.

> "I had to teach myself to like vegetables. Now I gotta have 'em every day."
>
> Rita, 17

Your Basic Smoothie

Wash, peel, and cut a variety of fruits you like into bite-sized pieces. Bananas, nectarines, melon, pineapple, mango, strawberries, and other berries work well. Store them in a closed plastic container in the freezer until they're frozen.

Pour a cup of liquid—100% fruit juice, skim milk, or water—into an electric blender. Add a mixture of the frozen fruits. Whip it up into a shake, and enjoy.

- ☆ Blending frozen bananas with milk (and cocoa powder if you want) tastes like a thick creamy milk shake with much less fat than real ice cream.

- ☆ Smoothies don't need any added sugar. The fruit provides enough on its own. If you want it a little sweeter, you can add some honey.

- ☆ Over-ripe fruit is good—it's even sweeter than normal.

What's my normal weight?

Only you can decide what your normal weight is. By paying attention to your health and how you feel—energetic, calm, wiped out, exhausted, or ready to go—you can tell whether or not you're at a healthy weight.

Doctors see hundreds of patients each month and usually use the optimum-weight chart developed by the Metropolitan Life Insurance Company to compare different people with different body types and metabolisms. Recent research, though, suggests that the "ideal" body weight for each woman is about ten pounds higher than what's on the weight charts.

No matter what the charts say, you're an individual, not a number. You have your own natural shape and body type. Maybe you're more muscular or more delicate, large-boned or lightweight next to your friends. You may be tall and thin or round or any combination of these things.

You probably know some young women (maybe even yourself) who have gone to great lengths, sometimes dangerous ones, to lose weight. Low-calorie dieting and diet pills are unsafe and can cause severe health problems, sometimes even death. At the same time, obesity is an increasing health problem for children, teenagers, and adults in the United States. Obesity brings along with it its own host of very serious health problems, including diabetes and cardiovascular disease. In 1999, the surgeon general warned that in the near future obesity will cause as many preventable deaths each year as smoking.

If you're feeling like you can't move your body the way you'd like to and want to lose some weight, try eating regular healthy meals and exercise—get your body moving to burn calories. This way, your body weight will set itself naturally.

> "When I was a teenager, my life revolved around my weight. I was on the bathroom scale three times a day. I finally shook it around 18, when I got more into exercise and healthy food and less into numbers."
>
> May, 19

> "Watching TV while I was growing up hit me hard because I was chunky but I wanted to be thin. I still want to lose weight and go down four sizes to a 14 but I don't have to go down to a size zero."
>
> Vivian, 17

How Can I Reach My Natural Body Weight?

☆ Experiment with what weight feels comfortable to you, rather than trying to be thin.

☆ Exercise and eat nutritious food to feel healthy, then let your body weight regulate itself.

☆ If you really want to diet, choose a program that emphasizes exercise and changing eating patterns, not starving yourself.

☆ Introduce changes to your diet slowly, one thing at a time so you won't feel overwhelmed.

☆ Think about your eating patterns over a one-week period, rather than food by food. Don't freak out about one day of high sugar or junk food.

☆ Try to make every bite count nutritionally. This means eating less junk food.

How do i know if i'm anorexic or bulimic?

ANOREXIA and BULIMIA are two eating disorders. They were most common among young white women until a few years ago, but now they also affect young women of color, young men, and people of all ages. Women who are anorexic slowly starve themselves through extreme dieting and fasting. Women who suffer from bulimia binge and purge—they overeat, then vomit or use laxatives, often in secret. An eating disorder is a very hard thing to have, and when they're severe, people can die from them.

> "I like to look at women's magazines because I get fashion ideas. But lately I've been noticing that after I read them, I'm kind of depressed and sort of panicky. Like I have to urgently go out there and do something to change myself. Usually to buy something."
>
> Elizabeth, 18

Eating disorders are very complex. A woman with anorexia or bulimia can't stop thinking about food or stressing about being fat—whether she is or not. But the root of the problem isn't really weight; it's emotional health. She may be stressed all the time, have problems with her family, friends, school, or have been sexually abused. Getting better means getting help with all of these problems, not just curing the eating disorder.

THINK

✳ Diet sodas are supposed to help you slim down, but the soda's artificial sweeteners can actually make you hungrier. Your brain thinks it's eating sugar and gets ready to digest food. When there isn't any, your stomach starts growling.

✳ Ever heard of a fat-free potato chip? In 1996, the FDA approved a fat substitute called Olestra for use in potato chips, tortilla chips, and crackers. Manufacturers claim there are no adverse health effects, but products made with Olestra carry the warning, "May cause abdominal cramping and loose stools." Sounds like bad news. The safest course is to avoid fake fats for the time being and gradually reduce the amount of fat in your regular diet instead.

✳ Most fat women believe that they eat more than their thin friends do. On average, though, fat people do NOT eat more than thin people do.

Source: Our Bodies, Ourselves

What can I do if I think my friend is anorexic or bulimic?

☆ Don't jump to conclusions. Make sure you've spent enough time with your friend to know that she has an eating problem. If she throws up once, she's probably just sick. If it happens every day, there's a good chance she's bulimic.

☆ Show concern and caring. Let her know you're there to talk.

☆ Remember that your friend's not crazy, she's coping with problems.

☆ Don't try to control her eating habits.

☆ Get help from a school counselor or nurse who knows how to help women with eating disorders.

☆ Not every nurse or doctor knows how to deal with anorexia or bulimia. If you don't feel confident about the help your friend is getting, support her in finding someone else to talk to.

☆ Call the National Association of Anorexia Nervosa and Associated Disorders at 1-847-831-3438 or visit their website: www.anad.org. They can give you a list of support groups and referrals in your area.

What are the effects of drugs?

Drugs and alcohol temporarily change your emotional mood, the way your body feels, and how your mind works. Habitual use can lead to psychological and physical addiction. You may end up craving the drug and needing it to feel okay. A lot of people think they have their addiction under control but usually over time a person will need to increase the amount of the drug they use to get the same feeling.

Sometimes in a family where there are already serious drug or alcohol problems, other family members will also turn to alcohol and drugs as a way to escape arguments, violence, and other craziness. Young women with strong support systems and fairly good communication in their family tend to use drugs less than others.

Sometimes young women use alcohol and drugs as a form of self-medication to ease stresses that they haven't found ways to cope with or work through, or to deal with emotional pain. Other times young women may just be curious and want to experiment with something new and different.

Studies show that young women and young men take drugs for different reasons. Young women often experience more pressure to act and look a certain way—to be nice and just go along with the crowd. Young women are sometimes told through movies and television that it is better to make other people happy than take care of themselves. You may take drugs to feel good when you feel bad about yourself because you're worried about being fat, skinny, or not pretty enough. You may take them because you want to do what your boyfriend's doing or because it's what your friends do when you all hang out. For some, a party isn't a party unless you get messed up.

Drugs and alcohol will alter your judgment and ability to make decisions. This puts you at risk of doing things you wouldn't normally feel

Elena's Story

I smoke cigarettes and weed with my friends most days, during lunch and after school. Hanging with my girlfriends, mostly. We used to cut out of science class after lunch. I never used any kind of needles, but I snorted smack a couple of times. Mexican stuff. Fucks you up. The thing I like about it is cuz I forget about the bullshit with my family. I don't feel like all the responsibility is mine then. Plus I like to party anyway, you know. Get trashed. I like hanging out with my boyfriend and his friends.

The thing I wonder about sometimes is about the future. But I don't expect to be alive then. I mean, in like, 20 years. I don't feel too good about lying to my mom, either. My dad, I don't care, he's drunk whenever he comes back to our house anyway. He's got another family too.

The other thing is that my body can feel it sometimes, like on Sunday morning, I feel like shit after coming down. My hair's kind of dry and my skin's getting old.

"Last Saturday I went to a party, it was a mini-rave. My boyfriend was going, and I wanted to be with him. Everybody was doing Ecstasy, and I felt like it too. It really makes you feel good and made me want to have sex with my boyfriend. But I ended up—there was this line of guys, and they all had sex with me. I guess I wanted to do it if I did it. But now I feel gross and really bad about it all. Was I raped? I don't even know what to think about it."

Alisa, 16

THINK

If you're going to try drugs, you'll want to know:

* Is the drug physically addicting?
* Can the drug cause short-term memory loss or damage?
* How much is safe to use?
* What's a safe place to use this drug?
* How long will I be high on this drug? What can I do if I want to come down sooner?
* How can I be sure the dealer is giving me the real thing? Where can I go to get the drugs tested to make sure they are not poisonous?
* Am I partying with people who care about me and who will take care of me if I get messed up?
* How can I protect myself from assault while I'm high?
* Or from stumbling in front of a moving vehicle?
* Or acting out of control and getting locked up?
* Will there be people who aren't getting high who will be in control if something goes wrong? Is there a phone to call emergency services?

comfortable doing. Alcohol and some drugs lower inhibitions. Because of this, drinking and getting stoned can make you feel more social, more flirtatious, more sexual. You might end up in social and sexual situations that you'd say no to if you were sober. This includes situations where your sex partner might have an STI or HIV.

If you plan on doing drugs or drinking, set things up so you'll still practice safer sex. Get into the habit of keeping condoms around and using one, even if you're trashed.

If you want to quit or cut down on your drug and alcohol use and have had trouble before, it may be good to work on one thing at a time. It's hard to quit everything at once. You'll need help. Surround yourself with the family and friends who support you. Change your environment to be around positive people instead of people who are using drugs, so it will be easier to stay away yourself.

Stop Your Cigarette Habit and Earn a Trip to the Caribbean!

It takes some scrounging to round up the money to buy a pack. In fact there are a lot of things that a one-pack-a-day smoker could buy instead of cigarettes, if she was willing to quit...

1 day = lunch out

1 week = three movie tickets

1 month = five CDs

1 year = trip for two to Cancún, Mexico, including airfare and hotel for a week

Drug Name	How It Makes You Feel	Some Side Effects
Alcohol: beer, wine, liquor, rum, vodka, whisky, fortified wine, malt liquor	Drinking it causes lowered inhibitions; puts you in a good mood, relaxes you.	Blotchy red face, vomiting, depression, lack of sexual arousal, aggressive behavior, blacking out, liver breakdown, brain damage, addiction.
Cocaine and Crack	Snorted, smoked, or injected. It leaves you with a hyped-up nervous energy, feeling of power and focus.	Depression, dizziness, smelly sweat, blurry vision, chest pain, insomnia, paranoia, the shakes, stroke, highly addictive.
Downers: barbiturates, sedatives, Quaaludes, ludes, Valium, Seconal, Nembutal, Rohypnol	Pills that give you a watery, relaxed, pleasant sensation, sleepiness, lowered inhibitions.	Mood swings, depression, crankiness, slurred speech, impaired judgement, loss of motor coordination. Rohypnol, the "date rape drug," puts you at risk for rape. Long-term addiction, and possible death.
Hallucinogens: Ecstasy, X, LSD, PCP, angel dust, mescaline, peyote, mushrooms, MDMA	Eating these pills, tabs of paper, or plant substances can cause intense sensory perception, pleasure, panic, hallucinations.	Dizziness, confusion, suspicion, higher heart rate and blood pressure and blood sugar levels, sweating, the shakes, flashbacks, depression, anxiety, possible heart and lung failure.
Inhalants: cement glue, spray paint, butyl nitrate, amyl nitrate, poppers	Sniffing or huffing it gives an instant rush for the brief time you're inhaling the drug.	Brain damage and damage to lungs, loss of muscle control, slurred speech, drowsiness, nose and eye secretions, possible death. (These effects do not apply to amyl nitrate, butyl nitrate, or poppers.)
Marijuana: weed, pot, grass, mota, bomb, bud, herb, ganja, thai stick, cannabis, hash	Smoked or eaten, it gives you a buzzed, relaxed feeling, can make everything seem funny, or deep, gives you a big appetite.	Blood-shot eyes, lack of initiative, paranoia, shortened attention span, bronchitis, decreased sex drive, short-term memory loss, addiction.
Opiates: heroin, opium, codeine, morphine, horse, tar, shit, smac	Snorted, smoked, or injected, it gives you a dreamy, relaxed feeling like floating.	Vomiting, clammy skin, sweating, low heart rate, physical addiction, loss of appetite, nodding.
Tobacco: cigarettes and chewing tobacco	Smoking or chewing it relaxes or energizes you, depending on how slowly or quickly you smoke.	Smelly clothes, breath, and hair, lung disease, heart disease, cancer of the lungs, mouth, and throat, emphysema, physical addiction.
Uppers: amphetamines, speed (methamphetamine or methedrine), crank, crystal meth, ice	Snorted, smoked, or injected, it makes you hyperenergetic, alert, fast, talkative, unable to calm down.	Crankiness, can't sleep, weight loss, stomach problems, sweating, bad body odor, extreme paranoia, addiction.

Why do we decorate our bodies?

Your body is a place where you can express your creativity with clothing, braids, a neck ring, an ankle tattoo, or a pierced tongue. You can ornament your body or paint your face, get rid of hair in some places or grow it out in others. By decorating your body, you assert your own personal identity and uniqueness. It also is a way to show that you belong to a certain culture, gang, or era.

We wear clothes to keep warm, but also to make an impression: to look tough, pretty, sexy, brave, formal, casual, classy. You may follow fashion or traditions, or break away with something new.

What is attention?

"Attention is when people listen to you or look at you. The kind of attention I like to get is when people are responding to what I say or do."
Rosa, 18

"I like compliments, when people praise me. When I dress up for a party, or when I change something about myself or try something new, I like it when people notice."
Trina, 16

"For me, negative attention is when you are thought of as a sex object. When someone says something like, 'You've got a big ass. I wanna hold onto it when I'm having sex with you.' When people make fun of the way you look. You don't want that negative attention."
Irene, 16

"Sometimes young women like to get negative attention from guys, cause they're not getting attention at home or anywhere else. Everybody needs attention, to be noticed."
Vicki, 15

Why do you dress like that?

"I like comfort. What I choose to wear has a lot to do with the weather. And I make sure that the clothes I wear don't restrict me."
Mika, 15

"I dress to impress—not others, but myself."
Thomishia, 15

"I try to look for things that nobody else wears."
Cyndie, 15

Natural Tattoos
by Lina, 18

When women want to celebrate their bodies, they choose a beautiful design to accentuate that. My clients want henna tattoos because they're fun. They also want to try something new, and at the moment, it's in style. A lot of my clients want a permanent tattoo, but they try henna tattoos first to see if they can actually live with the design.

Henna tattoos are natural and temporary. Henna is a plant that's ground into powder, then made into a paste that's applied to the skin, staining the body in patterns. It's an art that's centuries old. Some designs, like the Moroccan ones, are geometric, like triangles, arcs, and squares. In India, women decorate themselves with henna before a wedding, and the designs are more intricate. In Palestine, where my family comes from, countrywomen decorate themselves with henna for celebrations of all kinds.

I create most of my designs myself. They come from my imagination or patterns that I see in the world. I'll see tiles that have a nice design or patterns on a building. Some designs take me ten minutes to do. A dragon I once did took me two hours. Two years ago I wanted to travel to Europe. Making henna tattoos for people, I was able to earn enough to go.

I henna women, and sometimes men, at community fairs and art festivals. I also go to people's homes for henna parties. A group of women come, there's food and music, and they enjoy themselves.

Fresh Ink
by Jetzabel, 18

My tattoos are a way of expressing something to everyone around me. I get a lot of compliments on them. People appreciate your art. Because that's what it is—art. People tell stories with their tattoos. People who have full-body tattoos have their whole lives written on their bodies.

I think tattooing is good, because you're not worrying what other people say. You're conscious of yourself and what you want, and you're doing it. Just make sure you want that tattoo you're choosing. You can't get it, then change your mind.

Make sure that you get it somewhere you can cover it up if you have to. If you have one on your neck or forehead, people give you a hard time. Also, some businesses won't hire you if you have tattoos showing, even if you look presentable.

Some people look bad on you. They say, "Oh, my God! She's a gangster." I've heard that a number of times. But I don't have to be in a gang or in trouble with the law to have a tattoo. People that don't have tattoos, more power to them. It's a question of what you want to do to your own body.

What should i know before getting a tattoo or piercing?

The way an artist creates a tattoo is by inserting colored ink between the permanent base layer of your skin and the upper layer, which is constantly being shed. Here are some things to think about before you get a tattoo.

About the Tattoo

Although tattoos are removable, it's not easy and it's not cheap, so you might want to consider them permanent. Before you get a tattoo, take a moment to try to look at yourself in five, ten, or even 20 years. If you can imagine yourself happy with the tattoo that far into the future, go for it. If you're not sure, you might try a temporary tattoo first to see what you think.

About the Artist

Get a tattoo in a professional shop, rather than somebody's kitchen, a bar, or outdoors at a fair. But just because a tattoo artist has a shop doesn't mean the artist is professional. Check to see that your tattoo artist is a member of the Association of Professional Piercers (APP). Other certificates may not be valid. The shop should be as clean as a dentist's office. Feel free to ask to see samples of artwork so you can decide if you like the style.

About the Tattooing

Check to see that the artist wears latex gloves the whole time during the tattooing. Look around and see if disposable needles and ink spreaders are used. You never want someone to use a needle on you that's been used on someone else. Look for a recently serviced autoclave sterilizer—a machine that works like a pressure-cooker to kill any virus or bacteria on the equipment. In a reputable shop, all the inks will be fresh. They're poured into disposable caps for each customer and thrown away afterwards.

TIPS
Your New Tattoo

DO:
* Leave it alone
* Coat it lightly with Bacitracin ointment three times a day for a week

DON'T:
* Rebandage your tattoo
* Apply Vaseline or petroleum jelly or alcohol
* Let the tattoo dry out
* Scratch your tattoo or pick at it
* Expose it to sunlight for two weeks

What do i do if my piercing gets infected?

With any cut, wound, or piercing of the skin, infection is always a possibility. To prevent infection, stay away from swimming or soaking in a pool or hot tub until the piercing heals. Try not to play with your new jewelry, and keep it on, unless you want the hole to close up. Wash your hands as much as possible, and clean the piercing twice a day with warm water and an antibacterial soap.

If your piercing gets infected, hold a warm washcloth on the area for awhile so it can draw the infection out. If it really, really hurts and is red and warm, have it looked at. The doctor may need to give you antibiotics.

Dirty tattoo or piercing needles can carry sexually transmitted infections (STIs). Until your piercing is completely healed, the wound can be a point of entry for tetanus, hepatitis B, HIV, and other STIs. Keep your piercing far away from semen, other people's blood, and vaginal secretions until it heals. For some piercings, like belly buttons, healing can take six months or longer.

"Personally, I have tattoos and it's the worst mistake ever, because sometimes employers don't want to hire me even if I'm dressed nice. I don't think tattoos make sense for any young woman until she's of legal age and had some time on her own."

Irela, 17

What happens when i get my period?

Puberty will change the way your body feels and looks. While you're going through these changes, it's completely normal to have really mixed feelings about it, or to feel anxious, embarrassed, excited, or confused.

Though you'll go through basically the same stages as your friends, there are three billion variations of what is "normal." Same number as there are women on the planet.

During puberty, your hips will start to widen. It's very subtle, so you may not even notice this. Hair will start to grow under your arms and around your genitals, and finer hair begins to show on your legs, forearms, and face. Your breasts will start to change size and shape. This change may happen quickly or slowly, depending on how your body was designed.

You'll probably begin to sweat more, and you may start noticing acne or pimples. Sometimes the hormones of puberty can cause changes in your mood, making you feel more upset or excited about things than you used to. Don't worry—it's all normal!

What is PMS?

Natural changes in your hormonal and chemical levels in the week or so before your period can cause headaches and make you feel more tired, irritable, nervous, or depressed. Premenstrual syndrome, or PMS, is the medical term to describe many of these premenstrual symptoms.

The First Menstrual Cycle

Most young women will get their first period, also called the menstrual cycle or monthly bleeding, between the ages of 11 and 15. In some cultures and families, this is considered a time for celebration—when a girl becomes a woman. It also means that if you have unprotected sex, you're now able to get pregnant.

During your menstrual cycle a tiny egg is released from one of your two ovaries. This is called ovulation. The egg travels down the fallopian tube on its way to your uterus, or womb. This happens at different times for different women, but it's usually about two weeks before you get your period.

Meanwhile, your uterus builds up a thick inner lining of blood and tissue, getting ready for a fertilized ovum—that's a woman's egg after it's had contact with sperm. If the egg wasn't fertilized by sperm, you'll shed the uterine lining. The lining leaves the body through your vagina. This bleeding or menstrual flow lasts from three to seven days.

Keep track of your menstrual cycles. A cycle is the number of days from when you start bleeding—the first day of bleeding is considered the the first day of your cycle—to the day before you start bleeding again. The average cycle is 24 to 32 days. Some girls have regular periods. Other girls' periods are irregular—one time, it might come in 45 days, then the next time, maybe just two weeks later. Irregular periods can be confusing or annoying

> **"I got my period on my 11th birthday and I hated it. But my mom said it was a gift from God for my birthday."**
>
> Myrna, 19

but usually nothing is wrong. They're especially common in young women who have just begun to menstruate, but the cycles usually get more regular after a couple of years. If your period is irregular, and you're worried about it, have a checkup by a doctor or healthcare provider. Also be sure to see a gynecologist if you haven't had a period by age 16.

During your period, you may get cramps—pains around your lower stomach or back. These are contractions of your uterine and intestinal muscles caused by prostaglandin, a natural substance in your body. Some young women have severe cramping called dysmenorrhea, which happens when you have too much prostaglandin in your body.

How can i ease my menstrual cramps?

To ease some of the pain naturally, try drinking soothing tea, taking a warm bath, lying down with a heating pad, or getting a back massage. Orgasms can also help relax the uterine muscles. Over-the-counter drugstore remedies include ibuprofen-based capsules and tablets like Advil and Midol. If you're getting very painful cramps, your doctor may suggest birth control pills to make them milder.

> "Where I come from they say, 'If your body's naturally trying to get rid of something, it makes no sense to plug it up.' So I don't wear tampons."
> Elena, 15

> "I use tampons 'cause they're less mess and more comfortable. I change to pads at night."
> Jessica, 17

> "I'm not wearing diapers. I use tampons."
> Regina, 16

> "A tampon got stuck up there once. I was too dry and it hurt when I had to yank it out. So I stopped."
> Nicole, 19

Family Reactions

Adult relatives can have all kinds of reactions to the fact that you've gotten your period. Some celebrate it as the first step towards becoming a young woman. Others may let it pass without any noise. In more traditional families, your mom or grandma may consider it a secret between women. Some may even get worried or upset because it means you could get pregnant, or because it marks the beginning of the time you'll be becoming independent, when you'll need to be taking care of yourself. They may feel you need extra protection, and are afraid of the responsibility. Or they may be able to give good advice and help. However it goes with them, don't trip on it. You'll have your own feelings and thoughts about what getting your period means for you.

Tampons & Sanitary Pads

○ Sanitary napkins are long pads made of cotton or synthetic material with sticky flaps that help them stay put in your underwear. They absorb your menstrual blood.

○ Tampons are small cylinders of absorbent fiber encased in a cardboard or plastic insertion tube. They are inserted into the vagina to soak up menstrual blood.

○ Anyone can use tampons. It's a myth that you can't wear tampons if you haven't had sex yet. For most girls, the hymen—a thin membrane that stretches across the vaginal opening—already has holes large enough to slip a tampon through. If a tampon is inserted correctly, you won't even notice it's there. It's great to have a close girlfriend or female relative around for support and advice the first time you insert a tampon.

○ Both sanitary pads and tampons come in a bunch of different sizes and varieties. Some are meant for a light period, others for a heavier flow. You will need to decide which kind is the most comfortable and effective for you. For comfort and safety, you should use the smallest tampon that works for you and change your tampon every 4 to 6 hours.

○ After using a pad or tampon, wrap it in toilet paper and put it in the trash. Flushing pads down the toilet will definately clog up the pipes!

What happens at a gynecological (GYN) visit?

BODY

When should you go for your first gynecological (reproductive health) exam? Among doctors, family, and friends, there will be a variety of opinions. Some say go as soon as you reach puberty. Some feel you only need to go if you're sexually active or over 21.

Because the knowledge you get from a GYN exam can help you prevent cervical and breast cancer (which can even affect young women), and the exam checks to make sure that your reproductive system is healthy and free from infection, it's good to start early.

A pelvic exam is a general term for an exam of your vagina and cervix. Depending on how sexually active you are and what forms of birth control you use, a healthcare provider will recommend having this exam from every three months to once a year.

A Pap test (also called a "smear") is a specific test to check your cervix for cancer or cell changes that might lead to cervical cancer. This test is recommended just once a year.

Pelvic exams do not routinely involve testing for STIs. If you want—or think you need—an STI screening, request it from your clinician.

You may feel anxious about the exam, especially if it's the first time. Many healthcare providers know this and will help you through it.

How to get the best GYN exam

☆ Find a clinic that's teen-focused, or that sees lots of teens and young women.

☆ Many healthcare providers are friendly and helpful. But if you're not feeling comfortable with the service you're getting, ask for a different provider or find a clinic where you feel comfortable.

☆ If you prefer to be examined by a woman, tell the medical office that when you make your appointment.

☆ Feel free to ask your provider questions to learn more about the gynecological exam and what's going on while it's happening. This may make you feel more comfortable with the whole thing.

☆ If you've had sex without using a condom, definitely get checked for chlamydia, gonorrhea, and HIV. They're common among young people who've had unprotected sex.

☆ If you are examined by a man, there should always be a third person in the room with you.

Your exam will be done either by a doctor, a specially trained nurse, or other healthcare provider. It will include a pelvic exam, a Pap test and a breast exam, plus any tests for sexually transmitted infections (STIs) that you request or that are routinely done at the clinic. The clinician will probably ask you about your health and sexual history, so that she can give you the information you need most. She may talk to you about birth control options and/or give you referrals for other health services. She may also recommend STI tests, or you can request them yourself. You can be honest with your healthcare provider. She is not there to judge you or get you into trouble.

What happens during the exam?

If your gynecological exam is scheduled as part of an annual visit, a provider will greet you, then take your temperature, measure your blood pressure, and record your weight.

Next you'll be taken into an exam room, where she will ask you to get undressed and put on a special robe. She'll leave the room and give you some privacy to change. Before or after you undress, feel free to ask any questions you have about what's going to happen.

She'll come back and ask you to lie down on the examining table and put your feet in the stirrups (metal footholds) at the end of the table. She will look at your vulva—the area around your vagina—to make sure everything looks healthy. She'll wear latex gloves at all times.

Next she will put a speculum into your vagina. A speculum is a plastic or metal instrument used to hold the walls of your vagina open during the internal exam. Though it may feel a little strange, the speculum will only be in your vagina for a few minutes. If you're feeling nervous or uncomfortable during this part of the exam, talk to your healthcare provider about it. She should be able to give you some support and try to make it easier.

She will examine the inside of your vagina, looking at the color and texture of your vaginal lining and secretion. Then she'll do a Pap test, which is a swab of your cervix (the cushioned opening to your uterus located at the end of the vagina) with something that looks like a long Q-tip. Because the cervix has very few nerve endings, you won't feel much more than a little tickle. Cells on the swab are smeared onto a glass slide and sent to a laboratory to check for irregularities that could indicate cervical cancer.

After removing the speculum, the healthcare provider will put two of her fingers (her index and third fingers on the same gloved hand) inside your vagina, and she'll place her other hand on your lower belly. She'll briefly press on the inside and outside, checking to make sure your ovaries and other reproductive organs in your abdominal area feel healthy.

If you're sexually active, some clinics routinely check for STIs like chlamydia, gonorrhea, and syphilis. At other clinics, the healthcare provider may recommend some of these tests. The tests may be done by swabbing the inside of your vagina (like the Pap smear), or through a urine analysis. Occasionally, they may do a throat or anus swab for gonorrhea and chlamydia, too.

You'll also have a breast exam, and the health provider will show you how to do one yourself so you can do it at home each month (see sidebar). She'll feel your breasts for unusual lumps and bumps that could indicate breast cancer. More often, though, the lumps are not cancerous, but common conditions like cysts (small sacs filled with fluid), swollen glands, or fibroadenomas. Fibroadenomas are lumps that develop in your teens or 20s, do not fluctuate with your period, and are not pre-cancerous.

What is breast cancer and how can i prevent it?

In the United States, one out of nine women will get breast cancer during her lifetime. This year, a person will be diagnosed with breast cancer every three minutes, and die from it every 12 minutes. While it's more likely to show up in older women, young women do sometimes get cancer, so it's a good idea to get in the habit of checking your breasts every month. Most lumps you find are not cancerous, but it's important to have them checked out by a professional just in case.

How to Do a Breast Self-Exam

1. Do the exam at a regular time every month—say, a day or two after your period ends.

2. After taking off your shirt and bra, look at your breasts in the mirror.

3. Raise your arms over your head and check to see if there is any swelling or changes in the skin or nipples.

4. Put your arms at your sides and check again.

5. Put your hands on your hips and check once more to see if you notice anything unusual.

6. Lie down and put your fingers on one breast. Keeping your fingers flat, press the nipple and breast all over, feeling for lumps. Move your fingers in small circles over your breast and the area surrounding it.

7. After you finish the first breast, do the same for the second. If you notice any lumps or discharge from your breast, call your healthcare provider to discuss it. She may ask you to come in for an exam.

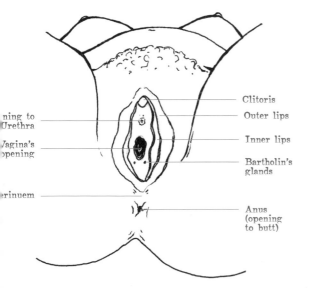

Female Genitals

Clitoris

Outer lips

ning to
Urethra

Inner lips

Vagina's
opening

Bartholin's
glands

rinuem

Anus
(opening
to butt)

What's going on down there?

You're probably noticing differences not only in your body's growth, but also in the kinds of natural fluids your vagina produces. You may notice new wetness, called secretions or discharge, about a year before menstruation starts. Here are some facts about what's healthy down there and what's not.

How do i know if i'm having abnormal discharge?

It's normal for women to have painless discharge from their vaginas. The vagina cleans itself through a discharge that is usually clear and thin—in fact, your vagina's one of the cleanest parts of your body. You may notice some wetness in your underwear or dried secretions.

Sometimes this discharge can signal to you that something's not quite right.

Signs of abnormal discharge are:

✔ a change in the amount, color, or smell of your discharge

✔ thick discharge that's white and lumpy, or gray, yellow, or greenish

✔ bloody discharge (not from your period)

✔ more discharge than you normally have

✔ itching in the vagina, or just outside it

✔ burning pain in your lower abdomen or stomach

If you're having any one of these symptoms, call your local health clinic, school nurse, Planned Parenthood, or doctor. Abnormal discharge can be the result of a yeast infection, bacterial vaginosis, or a sexually transmitted infection (STI).

What is a yeast infection?

Yeast is a natural organism usually present in the vagina in small amounts. But your system or your vaginal environment can get out of balance, and the yeast may grow too abundant, causing an overgrowth or yeast infection or another common infection, bacterial vaginosis (BV). These are very common in women and may be set off by unprotected vaginal intercourse with a new partner. Those who have HIV or immune system problems may get yeast infections more often.

Common signs of a yeast infection are:

✔ a white, lumpy discharge

✔ itching, often intense, inside or outside the vagina

✔ burning when you pee

✔ the lips of your vagina become bright red or inflamed

✔ abnormal smell

If you think you might have a yeast infection but it's your first time, call your health care provider to make sure that's what you have. Yeast infections can usually be cured within a week with creams or suppositories that you buy at the drugstore without a prescription.

TIPS

Some women use home remedies for treating yeast infections. Things that have worked for some women include inserting yogurt into the vagina, garlic suppositories, and taking cranberry concentrate supplements. Also, cutting down on sugar and caffeine and getting more sleep has helped many women prevent yeast infections from coming back again and again. But, if your symptoms don't go away, or get worse, you should go see your doctor.

Douche and Spray?

Douching does not work as birth control.

Vaginas clean themselves naturally through discharge, so you don't need to douche. Douching may upset the natural balance in your vagina and could cause an infection.

Feminine hygiene products are useless and can even be harmful to use, but make a lot of money for their manufacturers. Don't buy 'em.

Instead of douching, you can just clean your vaginal opening, vaginal lips and the area around them with warm water and mild soap when you shower or bathe. Vaginal secretions and scent are a natural part of womanhood. If you stay healthy and wash regularly with soap and water your smell will be just fine.

Medical providers strongly discourage douching at all. But for those who consider douching important: Do it rarely. Be careful not to use chemical douches, and don't douche too far up inside your vagina.

What is a urinary tract infection (UTI)?

Urinary tract infections (UTIs) are caused by bacteria that enter your urethra—the opening above your vagina where you pee from. The bacteria get into your urinary system, where your body processes urine and expels it from your body. UTIs can also be caused by other sexually transmitted infections.

UTIs are very common in women because the urethra is shorter than in men, making it easier for the bacteria to get into the urinary system. Sometimes UTIs can be serious. They usually occur in your urethra or bladder. If a bladder infection is left untreated, it may spread to the kidneys, which is very dangerous. You may be more likely to get a UTI if you haven't been eating well, have a weak immune system, have been under stress, or had surgery. Sometimes a sudden increase in sexual activity can cause a UTI. This is known as honeymoon cystitis.

Some signs of a UTI:

✔ burning when you pee, or urinate

✔ needing to pee a lot

✔ pain in your lower belly when you urinate

✔ your urine has a strong odor, looks cloudy, has a dark color, or has blood or pus in it

✔ you feel very ill, run a fever, or experience nausea, vomiting, or lower back pain— these can be signs of a kidney infection caused by an untreated UTI

Drinking lots of water can sometimes cure

UTIs that are bladder infections. The first time you have a UTI, call your healthcare provider to get more advice and to find out if you need to take medicine. After an examination, she will usually prescribe antibiotics. If you show signs of a kidney infection, you definitely need to call your doctor—drinking water alone won't cure it. If you have a UTI, avoid sex for a few days until the infection has left your system.

Preventing UTIs

TIPS

✳ Wipe from front to back. About 90% of UTIs come from E. coli bacteria from your anus, or butt, making its way into your urethra and bladder.

✳ Pee before and after sex, even when you don't feel the urge.

✳ Coffee, tea, and alcohol irritate the bladder. Pure cranberry juice without added sugar or cranberry juice extract (sold as pills at many health food stores) can sometimes help a minor infection. Drinking lots of water every day can also help prevent a UTI.

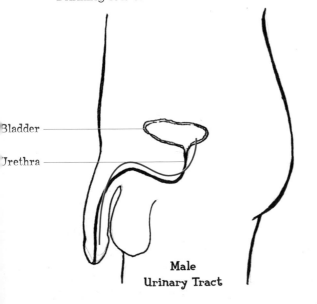

Bladder —————
Urethra —————

Male Urinary Tract

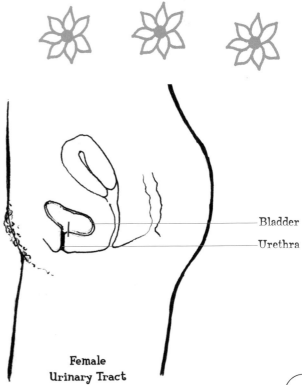

————— Bladder
————— Urethra

Female Urinary Tract

Blue line shows the length of the urethra.

How do i know if i have an STI?

Sexually transmitted infections or STIs (formerly called STDs) may be serious illnesses that can infect and damage your body's organs. They can be painful, and potentially make you infertile or even cause death.

STIs can be especially dangerous for young people. Often people show no signs of these diseases, and don't realize they have one unless they get tested. STIs are spread during oral, vaginal, and anal sex, and other close sexual activity.

STIs are spread by sexual contact because the bacteria and viruses that cause them survive in moist, warm areas of your body—the mouth, rectum, urethra, and vagina. STIs didn't used to be spread by sexual contact. Centuries ago the same bacteria infected colder, less homey parts of the human body, but mutated over time so that now they hang out and multiply in the body's warmest climate zones.

Getting Healthy Again

Most STIs are curable if you get treated. The worst part is learning that you have one. If you're like most people who find out they're infected, you're probably gonna feel guilty, scared, angry, or unclean.

You're not alone. Every day thousands of young women in the U.S. are told that they have an STI, and are making choices about how to take care of themselves. If you've got an STI, get support from a close friend and your healthcare provider so you can take the best care of yourself.

If you think you might have gotten an STI, go get checked. Follow these steps:

✔ *Get treatment,* no matter how hard it is or how bad you may feel. It's got to be done.

✔ *Call your local county health department* or family planning clinic for an appointment. Ask to make sure your visit will be private and confidential.

✔ *Follow the exact treatment plan your clinic worker prescribes.* Be sure to take all of your medicine, even if your symptoms go away before you're finished. When you stop short on antibiotics, only the weaker germs are killed. The stronger ones survive to make you sick all over again.

✔ *Tell your partner(s).* If you're still in a relationship and your partner is infected with the STI too, they can easily give it back to you. If you're too hurt or angry to talk to your partner, write a letter—even an unsigned one—or have a friend call.

Who Dunnit?

Anna and Tomas are both 18, and have been in a relationship for three years. Before they got together, each had a steady partner, plus a couple of affairs. Last week, Tomas found some thick yellow discharge coming from his penis. The doctor told him he had chlamydia. Anna went right away to the clinic. She also tested positive.

Now Tomas says he hasn't been with anybody else since he and Anna got together. He's pissed off and calls her a ho. Anna's mad at Tomas, too. She says she hasn't been with anyone but him. He's not just dissing her, she says, he gave her a serious STI that could make her sterile. And now she thinks he's lying to try and shift the blame. Choose which of these answers is what probably happened:

1. Tomas has been faithful. He got the STI from Anna, who's been sleeping with other guys.

2. Anna hasn't been with anyone else. Tomas has. And he's given her chlamydia.

3. Anna got chlamydia from a previous partner. But like most young women, she never had any symptoms and thought she was healthy. Without knowing it, she infected Tomas.

4. Tomas got the disease from a previous partner. Like some guys, he had no symptoms for a long time, and so he didn't realize he was infected or that he had passed chlamydia to Anna.

Answer: Any of the above. STIs often take a long to time to show up. Plus many people never show any signs at all. So it's hard to tell who's responsible or whether Anna or Tomas (or both) had sex with someone else. Playing around is one possibility, or either one could have picked up chlamydia from a previous partner, had no symptoms, and then passed it on. Anna and Tomas have some health and honesty issues to deal with. But for now, they need treatment.

Be real with yourself about whether you can trust your partner to tell the truth. Using condoms or not having sex are always the safest bets.

There are about 15 million new STI cases every year in the United States, and about a quarter of those infected are teenagers. Between 15-20% of young men and women are infected with herpes by the time they reach adulthood. Source: Centers for Disease Control

Chlamydia

How you get it: Unprotected vaginal or anal sex with someone who has chlamydia, or from mother to child during birth.

Signs and symptoms: Most women and half of men have no symptoms at all. Possible symptoms are a strange discharge from your vagina, bleeding between periods, burning when you pee, pain in your belly, fever, and nausea.

Effects: Chlamydia can lead to pelvic inflammatory disease (PID) in women, sometimes causing infertility. In males, it can cause permanently disabling arthritis.

Treatment: Easily treatable with antibiotics. Chlamydia is the most common of all bacterial STIs in sexually active young people.

Gonorrhea

How you get it: Unprotected sex in the mouth, anus, or vagina with someone who has gonorrhea.

Signs and symptoms: Half of women with gonorrhea have no symptoms. If you do, they show up from two to 21 days after having sex with an infected person. You may have a white or yellow discharge from your vagina, burning pain when you pee, abnormal periods, or stomach cramps.

Effects: Can lead to infertility, heart trouble, skin disease, and blindness.

Treatment: Curable with antibiotics.

Syphilis

How you get it: From kissing or unprotected sex in the mouth, anus, or vagina with someone who has syphilis.

Signs and symptoms: Syphilis goes through three stages. Most women show no signs. If you do, in the first stage you may get painless red-brown mouth sores three to 12 weeks after sex. These disappear after several weeks, but the syphilis remains. During the second stage, a week to six months after the sores heal, a rash and flu-like symptoms may appear.

Effects: In the third stage, syphilis invades other organs of the body and can cause brain damage, blindness, and death.

Treatment: Can be treated with antibiotics in the first and second stages. Syphilis is increasingly rare, but can be very nasty if you get it.

Pubic Lice/Scabies

How you get it: From sexual contact, or from other close physical contact.

Signs and symptoms: Severe itching. lice or eggs in your pubic hair. Scabies create reddish furrows under the skin in the genital area, buttocks, between fingers, in folds of your skin, under your arms, or on your feet.

Effects: Symptoms may get worse, lead to bacterial infection, or spread to others.

Treatment: Can be treated with over-the-counter or prescribed lotion and shampoos.

Genital Warts (Human Papillomavirus or HPV)

How you get it: Your genitals touch someone else's genital warts, but you can also get the virus when warts are not present.

Signs and symptoms: No symptoms, or small, painless bumps around your vagina or butt. Possible itching or burning in these areas.

Effects: Warts can get worse during pregnancy, making delivery difficult.

Treatment: Warts may go away by themselves, and if they do not, a doctor can remove them. There are many types of HPV, some of which have no symptoms. Remember that you can still be contagious even with no symptoms.

Hepatitis B

How you get it: From kissing or exchanging body fluids like blood, semen, or vaginal secretions through unprotected sex, sharing needles, or razors. Hepatitis B is 100 times easier to catch than HIV—the AIDS virus.

Signs and symptoms: Flu-like symptoms, fatigue, loss of appetite, nausea, yellowish skin and eyeballs, pain in the abdomen, light-colored feces.

Effects: Cirrhosis, liver disease, or liver cancer. Hep B can be fatal if you are a chronic carrier.

Treatment: There is treatment for the symptoms of hepatitis, but the infection doesn't go away. A simple three-step vaccination prevents hepatitis B.

Herpes

How you get it: From unprotected sex; any touching, including kissing, on your sex partner's herpes blisters; and from mother to child during birth. Open herpes sores are most contagious.

Signs and symptoms: No symptoms at all or small, painful blisters on the vulva, vagina, or near the mouth, one to 30 days after being infected. You may feel an intense tingling, itching, or burning just before the blisters appear.

Effects: Painful outbreaks of sores. Avoid sex if you're having a herpes outbreak.

Treatment: Herpes is a virus and can't be cured, but you can help ease some of the symptoms. Taking medication at the beginning of an outbreak can make it less severe.

TIPS

Cover yourself from the start. When you're playing around before sex, your partner's penis might be near your vagina and anus. If your partner has an STI, the pre-cum—the few drops of secretion that comes out of the penis before the guy ejaculates—is rich with STI sperm, bacteria, and viruses.

IF YOU ARE RAPED, forced, or pressured to have sex without a condom: ask for a test for HIV and other STIs. The tests are simple swabs or urine catches (for gonorrhea and chlamydia) or blood samples (for syphilis, herpes, and HIV), so they hopefully won't cause you any additional pain. To get more help for yourself after rape, see page 65.

What do i need to know about HIV and AIDS?

Human immunodeficiency virus (HIV) is a virus that attacks your body's immune system, the mechanism that fights off disease. HIV can severely cripple your immune system—that's when the illness becomes known as AIDS. For a healthy young woman without HIV, a cold or the flu is no big deal. But for a young woman living with AIDS, even simple illnesses can be life threatening.

Considering the growing numbers of young women contracting the virus, you'd think most doctors would be looking out for signs of HIV in young women patients. But they're not. In the early days, AIDS was thought of as a disease that only affected gay men and intravenous (IV) drug users. Many medical professionals (and many of us) are still behind the times—or in denial. "I'm not gay. I don't use IV drugs. My partner and I are clean. We're too young to get HIV."

HIV is here to stay, and anybody can get it. If you're sexually active or do IV drugs, it's a good idea to get tested—and to look out for the possible signs of HIV in women:

- ✔ frequent vaginal yeast infections
- ✔ swollen glands
- ✔ persistent dry cough
- ✔ skin rashes
- ✔ increase of genital warts or herpes outbreaks
- ✔ flu-like symptoms
- ✔ chronic fever, night sweats, headaches
- ✔ diarrhea, weight loss

HIV is colorblind. It's contracted through unprotected sex—vaginal, oral, or anal—with an infected person. Someone can get HIV by sharing needles with someone who has it, and it can also be passed from an infected mother to her baby. Gay, bisexual, and straight people all get it. White people get it, Black people, Latinos, and Asians. Young and old people get it. HIV does not discriminate. A lot of people who have it got it in their late teens.

HIV is a virus that breaks down your T-cells—the cells that fight off disease. Normally, we have hundreds of thousands of T-cells, but if you get infected, the virus kills them. Once your T-cell count is way down (under 200), your body can no longer fight off illness like it used to. Then it's easy to get diseases like TB and pneumonia. And even minor illnesses can become a dangerous problem. A person with HIV gets infections over and over again, and then it's called full-blown AIDS. Some people live only six months after they get AIDS; others for 18 years. It's a matter of taking care of yourself and a little bit of luck.

How do i reduce my risk of getting HIV?

Very low risk behaviors include masturbation, mutual masturbation, touching, massage, body-rubbing, kissing, and protected oral sex.

Low risk behaviors include deep kissing, oral sex, vaginal intercourse with a condom or female condom, and anal intercourse with a condom or female condom (try not to get semen or blood in your mouth or near broken skin).

High risk behaviors include vaginal and anal sex without a condom. Millions of people have gotten HIV due to these behaviors.

You cannot get HIV from someone's saliva, sweat, or tears.

- ✔ Being careful about sharing body fluids will help reduce your risk of getting HIV.
- ✔ Mixing drugs or alcohol with sex loosens your inhibitions and increases the chance you will take risks of contracting HIV.
- ✔ You can have any kind of sex you want and be safe from getting HIV, as long as it's safe and protected sex.
- ✔ If you're on the Pill, you're protected from pregnancy, not HIV or any other STI. To be safe, use a condom.
- ✔ Many people don't know if they're infected with HIV or not. Even if you're in a steady relationship, you and your partner might want to talk about HIV and get tested.

FACTS

- ✳ Worldwide, the highest rate of new HIV infection is among young people.
- ✳ Girls' rate of infection is higher than that of boys.
- ✳ The majority of young women with AIDS are infected during heterosexual encounters.
- ✳ In the U.S., 75% of young women with AIDS are Latina and African-American.
- ✳ Only 50% of youth reported condom use at last intercourse.

Think Positive

If you do test positive for HIV, it's extremely important to get a good healthcare provider and surround yourself with a supportive network of family and friends. You'll need to eat well and get plenty of sleep, and to cut down the stress level in your life. You'll still need to protect yourself during sex—with your immune system weakened, you'll be more vulnerable to contracting STIs and other illnesses. You'll also probably feel better knowing you're protecting your partners as well.

> **"**We're seeing a steep rise in the number of young guys coming in with HIV. They get themselves treated, we get it under control. The girls don't come in. They rarely get tested for HIV. I think we're sitting on a time bomb.**"**
>
> Nancy, a nurse at a San Francisco youth clinic

HIV Positive
by Mary, 18

I squeezed my boyfriend Jorge's hand. He turned and looked right at me. He looked more nervous than I was. I thought it was weird because he only had sex with me and another girl, and they lost their virginity together. I was certain that my results would be negative since Jorge was the only one I had ever slept with.

The counselor came in but kept her eyes down. She opened the folders with our names on them. She looked at them for a few seconds while Jorge and I focused on her.

"Well, your results for chlamydia and gonorrhea are negative," she began. "And you both tested negative for syphilis." I was relieved. I had never played around on Jorge and I knew in my heart that he would never mess with another girl behind my back. She got quiet then. She turned her body away from the desk and faced us. "But... you both tested positive for HIV." She began to tell us how we could take care of ourselves and what to do if we needed someone to talk to. She talked for about five minutes, and I really don't remember a thing she said. I wasn't listening to her anymore—I was numb. I didn't know what to do. She talked to Jorge mostly, because he was still listening, but he had tears in his eyes. He asked her a couple of questions. He seemed to be accepting the news so easily. She asked if I had any questions.

"Yes, I would like to know if the test was 100% accurate?"

"The test we do is pretty accurate, but if you'd like to take another one, you can. HIV usually shows up six months after a person has contracted the disease and sometimes not even then—a person could live a few years with HIV and never know if he didn't get tested." She looked at me. "I'm available to talk. In fact, I suggest we do. It's okay to be mad, sad, or hate this disease, but it doesn't have to equal death. If you take care of yourself and each other you can learn to live with HIV."

I tried to really listen to what she was saying, but I was so caught up in my own thoughts. I'm only 19. I'm still young and my whole life is ahead of me, and in the last few minutes, it was all taken away. Was Jorge keeping other secrets from me? I'd lost my virginity to someone I loved, someone I trusted. It just wasn't fair for me to be punished when I'd never done anything to anyone else.

Sometimes we forgot to use condoms, but I was on the Pill. We were faithful. He loves me, and I love him too. But now our dreams will never happen. How long can I live like this? Could I ever have a family? Why me? All these questions and more were running through my head, but I didn't feel like asking. Just knowing I was HIV positive was enough for one day.

Unprotected Sex
by Margarita, 24

Wanting too is infectious.
But the moment would be so precious.

If I could only take it.
And trust you to go naked.
To chance with all others you had
before me, and they before thee.
Is not worth my life's eternity.

Wanting too is infectious.
These moments can be contagious.
To say yes when I really don't know
would just be outrageous.

What happens during sex?

Sex is about a lot of things. The balance between physical and emotional pleasures and needs can vary a lot between people. There are lots of ways you can enjoy sex, and you also have the option to wait to start being sexual. There's no rush. It's your body, your choice, and your responsibility.

You may feel that you have to be sexy all the time and that image is everything. Or if you're not sexually active, you might be afraid of being left out. If you are having sex, some people might say you're a slut or a ho. You can create your own definitions and make decisions that are comfortable for you. Give yourself plenty of time—you may want to wait months or even years—to decide what you feel comfortable with. And you can change your mind whenever you want.

When you do decide to have sex with a partner, it's important to communicate and to share what you do and don't want to do. If you start having sex then decide to take a break for awhile, that's fine too. You're the only one who can make your own rules. It can help to figure things out by talking with a person you feel comfortable with.

Experts who study sex sometimes say that for human beings, the most important sexual organ is the brain. Enjoying sex fully has a lot to do with your state of mind. Having sex is best when you're with a partner who makes you feel strong, safe, and relaxed.

> "My girlfriend and I have been together for two years. We kiss and touch each other. We make sure to protect each other and ourselves."
>
> Misty, 18

> "The way it is at our school, you either have sex or you can't have a boyfriend. That's the way it is. There's lots of pressure. Maybe on the guys too. I think we should find another way."
>
> Yee, 16

Take Care of Yourself

If you have unprotected sex, you can get pregnant. So use birth control if you're having sex to enjoy it or to be close to your partner but not to have kids. (See pages 46-47.)

Sexual activity can also be harmful if it's not safe and protected. Know all you can about sexually transmitted infections (STIs) so you can protect yourself and your partner. (See pages 38-41.)

Why do some young women masturbate?

Masturbation is touching your own body to give yourself sexual pleasure. It can be a way of exploring and enjoying your body. Many women masturbate, most often by touching their clitoris, vulva, or vagina with their fingers, a sex toy, or a smooth object. Despite things you might have heard, masturbation isn't harmful. If your hands and sex toys are clean, you can't get an infection from masturbating and it doesn't affect any other part of your body in a bad way.

> "What I do is masturbate. I do it because it feels good, and I'm learning how my body works."
>
> Elizabeth, 19

If you do feel guilty or uneasy about it, though, you may want to stop and sort out your feelings before doing it again. Or you may not want to masturbate at all. There's no right or wrong about masturbation—it's just one more way of expressing yourself sexually.

What is an orgasm, and how do i know if i'm having one?

Rubbing, touching, or licking on or around your clitoris puts your body into sexual arousal. Sexual tension builds up. Orgasm is the point when all the tension is suddenly released in a series of uncontrollable, pleasurable, muscular contractions. You may feel the contractions in your vagina, uterus and/or anus, although you can have an orgasm without feeling any contractions at all.

You can experience many different types of climax. An orgasm may feel big and dramatic or small and relaxed, sensuous, intense, or awesome. An orgasm can feel different with a finger, penis, dildo, or vibrator in the vagina. It can feel different when you masturbate than when you're having sex with a partner. There

> ❝At my high school, half the girls are pregnant, but nobody's had an orgasm.❞
>
> Clarisa, 16

are all kinds of orgasms and all kinds of feelings that go along with them. What works, what feels good, and what is satisfying for you at any given moment is what counts.

Your sexuality develops over time. If you're sexually active and haven't had an orgasm yet, remember it can take a while to learn how your body works. Many women go a long time without having an orgasm. Some never have one at all. And some women only have them once in a while, or only when masturbating. Some research shows that women, unlike men, may have to learn how to have an orgasm, and that can take a while. You may be tempted to fake an orgasm to please your partner, but there's really no reason to. You can get really turned on and enjoy sex, without having an orgasm.

What about my partner?

Many guys don't know much about women's bodies so clue your partner in by explaining what feels good to you. If your partner is another young woman, she's likely to have a better idea of how the female body works because she's got one too. Still, everyone has different feelings and needs, and communication's the key to good sex, no matter who your partner is.

What do we do when we have sex?

There are a lot of ways to have sex. Penis-in-the-vagina intercourse is just one. In fact, this type of intercourse involves the least direct stimulation of the clitoris, the organ of sexual pleasure for many women. Experts say that other types of sex will bring you to orgasm faster and easier. Other kinds of sexual activity include:

Sexual fantasy—daydreaming about sharing physical pleasure with someone you know or an imaginary person. You can use sexual fantasy to get turned on and to help keep things going when you're masturbating alone or when you're having sex with someone.

Kissing a partner can be a very intimate experience. Some people feel it's even more intimate than intercourse. French kissing is kissing another person using your lips and tongue.

Mutual masturbation, or manual sex—when you and your partner stimulate each other's genitals or breasts with your fingers or sex toys to give each other pleasure.

Oral sex, or going down on a partner—when one partner licks, kisses, or sucks the clitoris and vulva or penis of the other. 69 is when two people give oral sex to each other at the same time.

Sexual intercourse—when a man's penis is inserted into the vagina and moves in and out along the vaginal canal. You can use other smooth objects to have intercourse with yourself or a partner, including sex toys like vibrators.

Anal intercourse—when a penis or sex toy is inserted into your anus. There are many STIs associated with anal sex, so use a condom.

THINK

Sexual Pressure

You may feel a lot of pressure to have sex from television, movies, or at school. But there's really no good reason why you have to have sex if you don't want to. Some questions to ask yourself about having sex:

✳ What do you want from having sex?

✳ Is sex painful or enjoyable for you?

✳ What do you like to do sexually?

✳ If you don't want to have sex but your partner does, how can you continue to stay close to your partner without doing something you don't want to do?

What is safer sex?

Safer sex is protecting yourself and your partner from giving infections and viruses to each other. It involves thinking about how you do sex in new ways because some sexual activities put you more at risk than others (see quiz below). You don't get HIV and other sexually transmitted infections because you've been bad. But they are out there, and you could get infected. The most common symptom of an STI is no symptom at all, so you or your partner could have one without even knowing it. STIs can cause serious damage to your body, or even death. And it takes only one contact.

The only truly safe sex is no sex at all. If you choose to have sex, then practicing safer sex means figuring out a strategy that will work for you—so you can enjoy and be more comfortable with whatever sexual activity you've decided to do.

Putting somebody else's pleasure before keeping yourself safe puts you in a risky situation for getting used, assaulted, or getting an STI. Pick up almost any women's magazine: the cover is bound to announce a quiz inside that will test if you know the secrets of pleasing your male partner sexually. Hardly ever a word about the real stuff: Being sexually active means communicating with your partner, and being responsible for your own body. You're too important to trust anyone else to take care of it for you.

A magazine sex quiz in which you and your safety really matter would ask:

✔ Can I talk about STI prevention with my sex partner?

✔ Am I able to hold off having sex with my partner if he or she won't cooperate?

✔ Do I feel comfortable trying out safer sexual activities?

QUIZ
Sexual Risk-Taking

Do you know which behaviors are the riskiest ones in terms of transmitting HIV and other STIs? Mark your guess—high risk, some risk, or no risk—then check below to see how much you know.

	High risk	Some risk	No risk
·Anal intercourse			
·Swimming pools			
·Sharing a drinking glass			
·Using drugs with needles			
·Abstinence (not having any sex)			
·Shaking hands			
·Vaginal intercourse			
·Oral sex on male with swallowing ejaculation			
·Oral sex on male without swallowing ejaculation			
·Oral sex on female			
·Fingering			
·Tattooing			
·Ear piercing and body piercing			
·Using your own sex toys			
·Sharing sex toys			
·Wet kissing			
·Mother-to-baby during birth			
·Receiving a blood transfusion			
·Toilet seats			
·Donating blood			
·Dry kissing			

"My boyfriend and I have been together for three years. We broke up about a month ago. He went to a party and had a one-nighter with this other girl, and got herpes from her. We got back together a week later. He didn't tell me cause he thought I'd break up with him. Now I've got herpes too."

Sandra, 17

Answers:
High risk—anal intercourse, using drugs with needles, vaginal intercourse, oral sex on male with or without swallowing, sharing sex toys, mother-to-baby transmission during birth, tattooing.
Some risk— oral sex on male without swallowing, oral sex on a female, fingering, ear piercing and body piercing, receiving a blood transfusion, wet kissing.
No risk—sharing a drinking glass, abstinence, swimming pools, using your own sex toys, shaking hands, dry kissing, donating blood, toilet seats.

Safer Sex = Communication with Your Partner + Taking Care of Yourself

You may eventually want a committed relationship where you can have unprotected sex without worrying about it. But that kind of relationship comes with time, and there's a good chance you could find yourself having sex before that time comes.

Condoms and Dams

Condoms are latex sheaths that cover the penis. When used correctly, condoms prevent transmission of STIs like HIV, hepatitis, and gonorrhea by providing a barrier between you and your partner's fluids. Condoms may not protect fully against herpes and genital warts since lesions and warts can crop up on other areas besides the covered ones.

To be safe, you should carry your own supply of condoms. Don't use a condom that a guy pulls out of his wallet (you don't know how long it's been there). And store condoms in a cool, dry place (like a dresser drawer, not the bathroom medicine cabinet).

How to put a condom on:

○ Try practicing on a banana first.

○ Check the condom for expiration date and air bubbles.

○ Pinch the condom at the tip to get out all the air. Leave a little extra space for the semen (cum).

○ Starting from the top, roll it all the way down to the base of the penis, being careful not to damage it with your fingernails.

○ Smooth it to make sure there are no air bubbles—they can pop and break the condom.

○ If it's a dry condom, add a water-based lubricant like K-Y jelly or Astroglide. Don't use oil-based ones like Vaseline because they can cause condoms to deteriorate and break.

○ Try putting a little lubricant in the tip of the condom before you roll it down. Your partner may find it feels more like the wetness inside a vagina.

Make putting on a condom fun. Try a bunch of different kinds of condoms: Lubricated for vaginal and anal sex, dry for oral sex. Try ribbed, ultra-thins, mint or banana-flavored, purple, green, or red. Condoms are sold as singles or packs in drugstores, and often you can pick some up for free at your local youth clinic. Try them all and compare to see which ones you and your partner like.

A dental dam is a square piece of latex that dentists use when they're working on your teeth. It can also be used in safer sex by stretching it across the vagina and vulva. Your partner can go down on you—lick or suck you—on top of this barrier without coming into direct contact with your skin. Glyde dams (available online at www.sheerglydedams.com) and ordinary plastic wrap can also be used in this way. You may like this if your clitoris is ultra-sensitive, because the stimulation is less direct.

It's not realistic to think that you could know all about your partner's former sexual partners. Your present lover could have slept with someone who slept with someone who slept with someone who was infected. Practicing safer sex means you respect yourself and your partner—not that the two of you don't trust one another.

Sex can be very exciting. You might want to try out new things and experiment. But you also might not want to deal with the reality of STIs. And chances are you might find yourself with a partner who doesn't want to deal with that reality either, and who asks you to have unprotected sex. It's a hard place to be. Are you willing to pay the price? Take chlamydia—it's the most common bacterial STI and 40% of those who have it are teenage women. In most cases, chlamydia has no symptoms, so you might not even know if you had it. But it can lead to pelvic inflammatory disease (PID) and leave you unable to have children.

If you already have an STI there are a few good reasons to still practice safer sex:

✔ You can easily pass it on to other people and harm them.

✔ If you have an STI like gonorrhea, genital warts, or herpes, you're at greater risk for contracting HIV because your immune system is down, and because the AIDS virus can more easily enter your body through the open sores.

TIPS

Five Safer Sex Strategies for Sexually Active Women

✳ Condoms help prevent both sexually transmitted infections (STIs) and pregnancy.

✳ Some sexual activities (like mutual masturbation or hand jobs) involve no risk of pregnancy and very little risk for HIV and other STIs.

✳ Having fewer partners and choosing partners who also believe in safe sex means fewer times you have to negotiate what you're going to do.

✳ Take it for granted that your partner might have an STI. Make a plan to protect yourself—the same way you would against getting pregnant.

✳ Get tested for STIs every six months, even if you're in a steady relationship.

What are my birth control options?

If you don't want to get pregnant, choose a method of contraception that works for you. The birth control options we have to choose from today are much more effective than the herbs and remedies women used in the past, but remember no birth control method is 100% effective except abstinence.

"Do you want to be a Dad?"

If you have a male partner, ask him this question. Most guys haven't thought that far ahead. Keep the words of one community health nurse in mind: "Sexually active young men also need to be active on the birth control front. You can protect and help your girlfriend. If you don't want to be a Dad, act like it. Do the birth control thing together."

"When I was 11, my 17-year-old sister had her first child. My mom told us that if we ever got pregnant after that, she'd kick us out of the house. That seemed easy to me. I'd never met a guy I was really close to, who I'd want to lose my virginity with. I thought I wouldn't have to worry about sex until I was at least 18.

"But a few years later, I met my boyfriend. It happened really quickly. We started dating and became a couple. Our attraction to each other was really strong. Soon we began having conversations about consummating the relationship. We really didn't think about all the consequences. I knew one thing for sure, though. I had plans to finish high school and attend college, and I didn't want a baby to get in the way of that."

Shirley, 18

THINK

Birth Control Is Individual

The type of birth control your girlfriend uses might not be right for you. A lot of young women stop using birth control because they don't like how it feels or the side effects it has on their bodies, so try to take some time and experiment to find something you feel comfortable with. You can choose your method of contraception based on your lifestyle and personal needs. Consider these questions when deciding which birth control method is right for you:

* Are you in a monogamous relationship?
* Are you a really organized person?
* Are you spontaneous?
* What will be a safe method for you?
* Does your partner have sex with other people?
* How often do you have sex?
* Will you feel embarrassed using this method of birth control?
* How do you feel about touching your body?
* Will your partner work with you on birth control, or will you be handling it yourself?
* Do you tend to have more than one sex partner?
* Do you need a birth control method that also protects against sexually transmitted infections (STIs) and HIV?
* Do you already have a baby?

My experience with Depo
Rosa, 17

I went to a clinic and talked to the nurse about getting on birth control, and decided to go on Depo Provera. A week later I got my first injection. For months, I loved it. I didn't get my period. I could eat anything I wanted and not gain weight.

Then I began having other symptoms. For a long time I didn't connect them with birth control: full-blown migraine headaches, a big decrease in sex drive. I basically never wanted to have sex, so there was no point in me being on the shot. Also, heavy mood swings. Often, when my boyfriend and I would get into fights, I'd end up crying or furious over something really little. Half the time I didn't understand it myself.

After nine months, I decided to go off Depo Provera. I had gained close to 15 pounds in two months time. I also broke out really bad and got my period for two months straight. Eventually, my headaches and mood swings went away. Now I finally feel like I'm myself again.

The morning-after pill, also called emergency contraception, can help you out of a jam. It must be started within 120 hours (five days) after you've had unprotected sex, and it reduces the risk of pregnancy by up to 89%. The morning-after pill contains a large amount of hormones that interfere with a possible pregnancy. You may experience nausea and vomiting. You can ask your healthcare provider for an anti-nausea medication. You can get emergency contraception from your regular healthcare provider, at Planned Parenthood, or a women's health clinic. **Or call 1-888-Not-2-Late for information about where you can get it in your area.**

Birth Control Method	What is it?	. Cost**	Does it work?	Pros and Cons
Abstinence	Not having sex	Free	100%	o No transmission of HIV or other STIs o Can't get pregnant
Barrier Methods: diaphragm and cervical cap	Provides a barrier so sperm can't get into the cervical canal	$20 plus cost of exam visit	84 – 94% * (cap effectiveness is much lower for women who have had a child)	o Only has to be used right before sex o No side effects o Can be used during your period o Have to use with contraceptive cream or jelly o Taste of creams can be unpleasant for oral sex o Need additional protection against HIV and STIs
Birth Control Pills	Synthetic hormones you take in pill form that stop the ovaries from releasing an egg each month	$5-35 each month plus cost of exam visit	92 – 99%*	o Must take pill daily o Simple to use o Rare risk of heart attacks and stroke o May cause change in weight, mood o Need additional protection against HIV and STIs
Condoms	Latex sheath that covers the penis and stops sperm from getting inside the vagina	$1 each	86 – 97%*	o Protects against HIV and other STIs o Easy to use and carry o Can buy in drugstores o Men have to participate o Can reduce sensation
Depo Provera	Injection of artificial hormones that stops ovaries from releasing eggs	$35 for three months plus cost of exam visit	99%	o Irregular periods o Lasts for three months o No advance planning before sex o Little worry of pregnancy o Must be injected by healthcare provider o Possible changes in weight, mood o May not be good for women with liver disease, blood clots, or breast cancer o Need additional protection against HIV and STIs
Female Condom	Small latex baggie with two plastic rings, the closed side covers the cervix and prevents sperm from getting in	$3 each	79 – 95%*	o Prevents against pregnancy, HIV, and other STIs o Woman has control o Covers more of the genital area than male condom o Man does not need to maintain an erection o Messy o May slip around
Fertility Awareness Methods	Observation of your body's changes and fertility to understand when you can and can't become pregnant	$10 for the thermometer	75 – 99%	o Have to be comfortable with your body o Need to take your temperature every day and write it down o No side effects o Need cooperation with sexual partner o Risk of pregnancy if you don't do it correctly o Need additional protection against HIV and STIs
The Patch	A plastic patch worn on the skin releases synthetic hormones that stop ovaries from releasing eggs	$30-35 a month	92 – 99%	o No advance planning before sex o Can be removed when you want a pregnancy o Only need to re-apply once a month o May not be good for women with liver disease, blood clots, or cancer of the breasts or uterus o Need additional protection against HIV and STIs
The Ring	A small, flexible ring inserted into the vagina once a month. The ring releases synthetic hormones that stop your ovaries from releasing an egg.	$30-35 a month	92 – 97%	o No advance planning before sex o Can be removed when you want a pregnancy o Only need to re-insert once a month o May not be good for women with liver disease, blood clots, or cancer of the breasts or uterus o Need additional protection against HIV and STIs
Spermicidal suppositories, foam, and film	Sperm-killing chemicals placed close to the cervix in your vagina	$10-$12 per tube	71 – 85%*	o Need additional protection against STIs o Easy to use when you need it o Must be used shortly before sex o Can irritate the skin of the vagina or penis o Should not be used many times a day
Withdrawal	Removing the penis from the vagina before ejaculation	No cost	73 – 94%	o Not an effective method of prevention of HIV and STIs

** These costs are approximate and will vary.

* Effectiveness varies based on correct usage every time.

What can i do if i get pregnant?

Getting pregnant can be a wonderful and exciting thing. But if you didn't plan for it, you have a potentially difficult decision to make. Talk with people you trust, and take time to think about your options and what you want so that the decision is one that you can live with. If you are pregnant, your options in the United States include medical or surgical abortion, or carrying the pregnancy to term to keep the baby or give it up for adoption.

How do I know if I'm pregnant?

If you're sexually active and have any combination of the following symptoms, you may be pregnant.

☆ **Nausea or sickness in the morning or other times of the day**
☆ **Soreness or swelling of breasts**
☆ **Unusual weight gain**
☆ **Spotting in underwear**
☆ **Fatigue**
☆ **Increased appetite**
☆ **Emotional highs and lows**

You can test yourself at home with a drugstore pregnancy kit, or you can go to a Planned Parenthood office or women's clinic and have a healthcare provider give you a test. If you discover you're pregnant, talk to a counselor whom you trust—discuss your feelings and goals for your life. Think over your possible futures. What you decide could change your life. Some questions to think about:

☆ **Am I ready to offer all my energy to parent a child?**
☆ **Do I have the money to support a child?**
☆ **Do I expect others to pitch in financially? Will they?**
☆ **What does it mean to have responsibility for another person?**
☆ **What would I do if the father leaves?**
☆ **What am I doing for myself and my future right now?**
☆ **What do I want for myself in five years?**
☆ **How do I feel about abortion and why?**
☆ **How will I find a way to take time for myself?**
☆ **What kind of support network do I have to raise a child?**
☆ **If I have a child, will I have to stop going to school?**
☆ **Do I expect my family to help me take care of a child? Will they?**

Options for Dealing with an Unplanned Pregnancy

The length of time for choosing between having a baby or having an abortion varies depending on where you live. Keep track of the date of your last period, because the sooner you make your decision, the more options you have.

Abortion

Before 1973, abortions—except those done to save the mother's life—were illegal in most of the 50 states. Many women died from unsafe illegal abortions. Then a woman who called herself Jane Roe challenged the abortion laws in Texas. The U.S. Supreme Court heard her case and ruled that banning abortions violated women's constitutional rights, especially their right to privacy. This famous case, Roe vs. Wade, made history. Women's right to decide when and if they wanted to bear children is now protected under the law.

Each state has different limits on how long you can be pregnant and still have a legal abortion. Unfortunately, many young women delay their decision, either out of shock at being pregnant, because it takes too much money to get an abortion, or because they are unsure of their rights. If abortion is the option you're choosing, it's important to act quickly—the physical, emotional, and legal process will be much easier for you.

Medical Abortion. For up to nine weeks after the onset of your last period, you may be able to end your pregnancy by taking a combination of drugs, dispensed by your doctor or clinician. Although there is usually severe cramping, many women find this preferable to a surgical abortion, because it doesn't involve surgery or anasthesia, and it may feel more private (part of it can be done at home) and comfortable than a surgical procedure.

Did You Know?

Many "Crisis Pregnancy Centers" listed in the phonebook are not what they claim to be. These centers, sometimes called "Pregnancy Aid" or "Pregnancy Counseling Centers," are designed to mislead young women. They are anti-abortion centers and try to talk young women out of getting abortions. Many of these centers offer free tests but have no doctors or nurses. They also insist that you come in person to talk. Beware. To be sure you get the help you need, call one of the numbers listed in the resource section of this book.

Surgical Abortion. During a surgical abortion, a woman's uterus is emptied by a vacuum-like machine or other instruments. The procedure can be painful for some women, and many get cramps afterwards. During the abortion, a woman will have the choice to either take drugs or a local anesthestic to help dull the pain. In most clinics, she'll receive counseling before and after the abortion to make sure she feels comfortable with her decision. It's a good idea to have a friend along for support, and to help get you home.

Adoption

If you decide to give birth to a baby but feel you are not ready to be a parent, you may decide to give your baby up for adoption. This means that you give up your legal rights as the baby's parent. Usually adoption means you're permanently separated from the child. Depending on the agency that handles the adoption, though, you may or may not have some say in who your baby will go to, whether you can visit your child, and if your child can contact you when she grows up. Ask about these details when you talk to the adoption agency.

Carrying the Pregnancy to Term

If you decide to have a baby, it's important to get prenatal care early on in your pregnancy. Young mothers are often late in getting healthcare. This can cause problem pregnancies, low birthweight babies, and a higher risk of miscarriage—although miscarriages are not unusual and can happen in at least 25% of pregnancies and can occur for reasons beyond your control.

As soon as you discover you're pregnant, all alcohol and drug use must stop. Drugs can lead to terrible health problems for your baby. When a pregnant woman uses addictive drugs like heroin, her baby may be born addicted and experience drug withdrawal. Drinking during pregnancy can cause Fetal Alcohol Syndrome (FAS). Kids with FAS may have abnormalities in their growth, in the formation of their organs, and in their neurosensory system. FAS is also one of the leading causes of mental retardation.

THINK

Legal Issues

Here are some of the legal terms you need to know and a list of the states that require you to tell your parents if you want to have an abortion.

Parental consent: You need to get permission from a parent or sometimes both parents, to get an abortion if you're under 18 in: Alabama, Arizona, Idaho, Indiana, Kentucky, Louisiana, Maine, Massachusetts, Michigan, Mississippi (both parents), Missouri, North Carolina, North Dakota (both parents), Pennsylvania, Rhode Island, South Carolina, Tennessee, Wisconsin, and Wyoming.

Parental notification: You need to tell a parent in writing, but you don't need your parents to agree, to get an abortion in Arkansas (both parents), Delaware (if you are under 16), Georgia, Iowa, Kansas, Maryland, Minnesota (both parents), Nebraska, Ohio, South Dakota, Texas, Utah, Virginia, and West Virginia.

Judicial bypass: In all of the above states, if you feel you can't or don't want to involve your parents, there are ways to get an abortion without their knowledge. You can talk to a judge and the judge can decide if you are mature enough to make the decision or if the abortion is in your own best interest.

These states require no parental notification or consent, or the laws involving parents have been declared unconstitutional and are not enforced: Alaska, California, Colorado, Connecticut, Washington D.C., Florida, Hawaii, Illinois, Montana, Nevada, New Hampshire, New Jersey, New Mexico, New York, Oklahoma, Oregon, Vermont, and Washington.

State laws are always changing. Many of the states that don't currently require parental involvement used to. The most up-to-date laws in your state can be found by calling a clinic like Planned Parenthood. These clinics can also help with the process of getting a judicial bypass.

Note: Anyone can legally buy a home pregnancy test at any drugstore or supermarket.

Having an Abortion
Nicole, age 19

Every morning the same thing happened. I had morning sickness—so sick to my stomach that I would be scared to get out of bed because I'd throw up. I was sick of being sick, and knew I wasn't ready to have a baby at the age of 16.

I was going to the clinic to have an abortion. My boyfriend's mother helped me arrange it and was by my side with my boyfriend. I needed to be there at 9:30 am with an empty stomach. I was given some pills to relax and a gown to slip on, then the nurse had me lay down.

She gave me a shot to numb my cervix. The pills started to make me very drowsy. The nurses inserted a tube into my vagina and turned on the machine. I felt a sharp pain. I was so tense that I felt as if the pills didn't have any effect on my body. The doctor rotated the tube in a circular motion, and I felt my stomach squeeze. I felt some sharp pain. It lasted about 30 minutes.

I felt guilty and really sad for the loss sometimes. Other times I felt strong and brave. But in the end, I do feel it was the right decision for me. I was sad, but proud of myself for doing the thing I needed to.

What's it like to be a young mother?

What happens to my body after i have a baby?

Your body and emotions have been through a million changes and you're probably pretty exhausted.

After your baby is born, your uterus will begin to return to its former size—shrinking from an organ of about three pounds to one weighing about two ounces. You'll need to massage it for the first ten days or so. There may also be a lot of vaginal discharge as the uterus sheds its thick lining. You may experience strong cramps or "after pains." Relaxing and breathing will help.

Your period should return anywhere from three weeks to several months after your baby is born. You can get pregnant again very soon after giving birth: many sexually active women (85%) become pregnant in the first year after giving birth if they do not use birth control.

Milk will develop in your breasts, so you'll need to keep them extra clean. Your breasts may be very sore, cracked, or raw. Ointment can help relieve the pain. If the skin below your vagina was torn during birth or the doctor performed an episiotomy—cutting of this area to make it larger—the tear or stitches will need time to heal.

You'll need to drink plenty of fluids if you're breastfeeding and eat extra protein, just like when you were pregnant. Eat foods rich in vitamins B and C, iron, and calcium, like cheese, meat, whole grains, and orange juice.

Don't Go it Alone!

Who can you count on? As a young woman with a newborn baby, your support network can mean the difference between constant crisis and a sane life.

Friends and family can be lifesavers. You can also learn a lot from spending time with other young mothers who are going through the same things you are. Many community organizations and women's centers have groups for teen mothers to help with child care, share parenting advice, talk about job leads, and learn how to cope with your feelings.

You might also want to spend some time with your friends who don't have kids. Taking a breather from talking about diapers and feedings can be good. Catching up on the news about school, your friends, and music helps to keep you in touch and feel less isolated and stressed out.

What's the Picture I'm Painting?

An Interview with Talena, 16

It's hard being a single parent when you need a break, or when you're in a financial bind. The nice part is that you have a part of you on this earth to cherish and guide through good and bad times. But you go through a lot of depression. You're constantly keeping your eyes on your child to make sure she's safe. And you go through a lot to find a willing babysitter so you can go to school or work to support your child.

Sometimes I think about how different my daughter's life would be if her father was around. Still, he's the one who chose to miss out on this precious time of her life. Raising my child alone has advanced my parenting skills and made me a stronger woman. My child motivates me to keep going when things are at their worst. No one else is going to provide for my child's needs. So I never give up. That would be letting her down, instead of teaching discipline and motivation.

Looking back, I'd have waited to have a child. Juggling school, jobs, and a baby leaves me no time for myself. My mother told me, but all I saw was my other friends with babies. I though it was cute. I didn't see the consequences. Right now, I'm working after-school jobs to support us, but it's just not enough to get by.

A young woman needs to think hard about the future she's planning. By having a baby, she's losing her teenage years to fulfill a dream she may lose tomorrow. It forces her to drop what she wants to do in order to parent a child full-time. She needs to ask herself, "Is this the picture I'm painting?"

"When I got pregnant I was nervous. I couldn't wait to see my baby. I'm happy now but it's hard when you're younger because you have to think as an adult does. I got help from my family and his family, which has made a big difference."

Katherine, 19

Team Work

In a big apartment block on the outskirts of the city live ten young moms raising babies on their own. Talking together in the basement laundry room, they realized they all had problems putting together enough money for big expenses: Leticia, for example, wanted to buy a sewing machine. Dora wanted to buy her seven-year-old boy a real bed. Tania needed to go to the doctor, but couldn't afford it. All the women were struggling just to meet daily expenses. Then Leticia had an idea: Every month, each of the ten women would scrape together $20 and put it in a pot. The collected money came out to $200 in all. Each month, one of the ten women would have her turn to take all the money home at once. This way, each woman was able to make the big purchases she needed to.

"The thing is that I was really good at English before all this happened, before the baby came, when I was in school. Other subjects too. I wanted to become a teacher, and I still do. But that's a long time from now. One day. My mom told me as soon as I had the baby, I had to move out. And right now, it's just about finding a sitter to go to the store, and getting Jason his medication. He needs to take it three times a day. And I need to make sure that he doesn't fall down, or get hurt. He's fragile and needs a lot of care."

Mary Elizabeth, 18

"What's a typical day? Katy and I get up in the morning, and every day we fight about the same thing—candy. She wants candy. And these days she'll holler for 45 minutes straight unless I give it to her. Then I get her fed and dressed and try to clean up a little and then I go off to school. In the afternoon we go for a stroller ride, usually to the park. I'm sick of it. Katy likes the slide so we go. Then we go home and I make us some dinner and try to get her down. She won't go to sleep without me so I always stay and sometimes I fall asleep myself. That's what my life is, day in and day out."

Krystal, 17

"I love my baby but it's not what I pictured it to be. I don't feel 16. Not like my friends feel at 16. I pay the rent, I buy the food. I'm nervous all the time. I expected Jaime would stay with us and help out but it went bad since the middle of my pregnancy. We tried for awhile. But he would bring his friends by and they'd be drinking and smoking and mistreating me. Then I found out he was sleeping with other girls too. One of them has a baby girl by him. When he told me he was moving out I was hurt but I wasn't sorry. We'll make it on our own, somehow."

Laura, 16

What is a healthy relationship?

Whether you're talking about a relationship with family, friends, teachers, boyfriend or girlfriend, a healthy one has got to be about R-E-S-P-E-C-T. From there, the terms of a relationship can vary depending on how close you are and what the circumstances are. A teacher-student relationship, for instance, has more distance and boundaries and fewer emotional ties than a friendship or the bond between you and your mom. Your relationship with your honey is sure to have a different feel than your connection to your little sister or big brother. But they all have to have some level of respect to be good.

> "My boyfriend and I are totally different. He likes to be laid back and chill out at home and rent a video, but I like to go out. We're into totally different movies and foods. We fight sometimes, so we can get our voices out there.
>
> But we also compromise. He introduced me to Japanese food, he reads the newspaper a lot and keeps me up with what's really going on. I've shown him different things I learned working at nonprofit places—like how the city is run and how the budget is handled.
>
> We're always learning new stuff about each other, like how he's been to seven different states, and he learned about my little sister who was paralyzed from the waist down and no longer lives with us. We talk about things and I guess I just treat him like he's my best friend."
>
> Shirley, 17

What's Up With Us? QUIZ

If a relationship is giving you the creeps for any reason, it's worth stepping back and looking at why. Any kind of relationship—heterosexual, lesbian, friends, employer-employee, teacher-student, or parent-child—can be unhealthy. Think of a relationship that doesn't feel quite right and ask yourself these questions:

1. Do I feel scared or nervous around this person?
2. Do they put me down or humiliate me?
3. Do I feel pressured or controlled by this person?
4. Is this person super jealous in a way that is scary, like maybe checking up on me, following me, or intimidating me?
5. Does this person threaten to kill themself if I break up?
6. Am I constantly blamed for their mistakes or temper tantrums?
7. Do they call me names or tell me that I need to change?
8. Am I desperate to be with this person, even to the point of flaking out on important jobs or duties just to get together?
9. Does this person hit or slap me?
10. Do I feel like I'm addicted to this person, or like I'm just killing time until I can see them again?
11. Does this person demand sex to show that I love them?
12. Do they insist on not using a condom or having unsafe sex or otherwise putting their pleasure ahead of my safety?

Answers:

If the answer to even a few of these questions is "Yes, most of the time," you may be in an abusive relationship and may need to take steps before things get any worse. Most abusers do not change on their own. "Yes" answers to questions 8 and 10 suggest that you may just be too wrapped up in the relationship and may need to pull back. Being obsessed with your girlfriend or boyfriend can be harmful and very painful for you. It can also make your partner feel suffocated and threatened.

Signs of a Healthy Relationship

- You feel free to be yourself around this person.
- You both accept each other's differences.
- During disagreements, you both make an effort to talk things out honestly.
- You are both willing to compromise sometimes.
- You don't feel guilty or pressured by your partner.
- You generally feel appreciated and liked.
- There's no verbal, physical, sexual, or financial abuse going on.

How can i get out of an abusive relationship?

Tell your parents, a teacher, or another adult whom you trust.

Avoid being alone with the abusive partner. And if you are alone with your partner, always try to have an escape plan—carry money for a bus or a taxi home, and have an excuse ready if you want to leave a situation. Tell friends and relatives about your situation so that they can come pick you up or screen your calls.

Join a support group for young women in abusive relationships. Breaking up with an abusive partner is just the first step in breaking out of the relationship.

If you're ready to end the relationship, break the news to your partner on the phone or in a public place where you feel safe.

Call the police if your partner threatens or attacks you. The only legal way to keep this person away is to get a restraining order and call the police every time they attempt to contact you. *Call 911 for the police or 1-800-799-SAFE for the National Domestic Violence Hotline.*

The Cycle of Abuse

Many abusive relationships have intense highs and lows. For instance . . .

- At first, you're both "lovey-dovey" and blind to each other's flaws.
- Then your partner starts getting moody while you try to keep them happy.
- Eventually your partner blows up and hits you or goes off on you verbally.
- Then your partner feels guilty, tries to make it up to you and promises to change.

Then the unmerry-go-round starts all over again.

I Got Out Okay: Isabella's Story

I met my first boyfriend when I was 15. He was three years older. At first he came across as pretty nice towards me, sort of protective of me.

But it wasn't long after we got together that he started this jealousy thing, like he was constantly watching me to see if I was cheating on him. He just went crazy if I talked to other guys at a party. He said, "You're my girlfriend and you do as I say." At the time, I took it as a sign that he really loved me.

We slept together after about a month. I didn't really want to do it. It was my first time and I was really stressed out about it, but I thought I'd better, because he really wanted it. He'd say, "I don't think you really love me." Eventually I gave in to the pressure.

There was only one time he actually hit me—when I talked back to him, he slapped me. But all the harassment and criticism just wore me down. Normally I'm a really talkative person, really social and happy, but I became really quiet with him, hardly ever smiled. I was just so stressed out all the time.

Once some friends saw him shouting at me about something and they said, "Why do you put up with it?" That made me feel really bad too, because I felt so stupid, like there was something wrong with me for putting up with it. But I just couldn't leave him. I thought he really loved me.

This went on for nearly three years. Finally I decided I had to break up with him. One day, I was late to meet him because I was working on a class assignment. He was so angry I was late that he grabbed the assignment and ripped it up. I said, "That's it," and I walked away. He said, "Don't you walk away from me." So we screamed at each other in the street. He grabbed me by the arms and said if I left him he'd tell my parents that I've had sex. But I just didn't care anymore. I thought, it'll be easier to deal with my parents' reaction than to stay with him.

When I got home I just burst into tears in front of my mother. She was pretty shocked, saying, "How could you? You should have told us." Then there was a knock at the door. My dad answered it, and it was my boyfriend. Dad wouldn't let him in, so my boyfriend started yelling at him. Dad managed to get the door shut to keep him out.

He didn't come to my house again after that—I think he was scared about my parents calling the police. But for a while he kept turning up after school and would come up to me and either shout at me or plead with me. I'd told a few school friends, and they were really good about it. It was such a relief to tell people. I felt so much stronger.

And even though it took a while to start trusting people again, it eventually made me stronger and more aware of my rights. Now, a year later, I've got a boyfriend who really respects me. He never pressures me, and I can be myself with him. Now I know no one has the right to treat me like that. At the first sign of control or manipulation or pressure, it would be like, I'm out of here. If you love someone you show them respect.

(This story is from the Domestic Violence and Incest Resource Centre in Victoria, Australia.)

How do i know if i'm in love?

Love can allow you to feel deeply connected to another human being, accepting who they are, and discovering more about yourself in the process. It can be about wanting to nurture someone else and feeling nurtured yourself in the process. It can be dizzying and scary at first. Many new, intense experiences have that effect. But if the feeling of being in love lasts, it can also be comforting and calming.

There is a difference between loving someone and being in love. Although both can open you up to some incredible experiences, what is called being in love often is more like infatuation—when you think about that person all the time and can't imagine not being with him as much as possible. When you're infatuated with someone, you often don't notice the flaws and you're willing to put everything—and everyone else—on the back burner.

If your relationship lasts past the infatuation stage, you'll find that you will begin to come back down to earth. Instead of feeling "head over heels" you'll be more aware of what's going on inside. You may care deeply about your partner, but you stop trying to rearrange your life around that person. Instead, you'll both start learning how to fit each other into your everyday lives. This kind of love is more nurturing and accepting, less trippy and possessive. This kind of love can survive those first challenges.

If you're experiencing some first-time feelings in a relationship, here are some questions you might ask yourself to find out if it's love: Do you feel lit up, energized whenever you see that person or hear their voice? Does just knowing this person make you feel full, satisfied, and happy? "Yes" means you're probably in love. So kick back and enjoy it.

> "When I asked my friend to become my girlfriend, I knew I was in love. In the past, my relationships were always based on sex. But this relationship was different, it felt like something more. We finally did have sex but since I loved her, it made sex so much sweeter. So basically, I knew I was in love because I did not base everything on sex."
>
> Yolanda, 16

> "I knew I was in love when my boyfriend had told me he was going on a college tour. He would be away for about ten days. But even though he was gone, I was still warmed by his presence. When you're in love, miles do not separate you."
>
> Amira, 17

> "Love is the concern for the best in the life of the one you love. If you can say that for someone, then you're in love."
>
> Adriana, 16

> "I knew it wasn't love because most of the time we were around each other, he would be getting on my last nerve. The only time he wasn't was when he was buying me something or at least talking about buying me something. I guess if you're truly in love, you cannot wait to be embraced by his presence and you care about him as much as you care about yourself."
>
> Nicole, 15

> 66 Sometimes you don't know you're in love until you lose that person. 99
>
> Seoufa, 17

Not Exactly Love

I want you around

because you're the only one

there for me.

Your shoulder is always there

to cry on.

But this isn't love,

it's only loneliness

tapping me on my shoulder.

Jessica, 16

How do i deal with a breakup?

So you just got dumped—your relationship is over. What do you do?

It's bound to hurt at least a little, so give yourself some time to feel sad or angry or humiliated. You'll also need time to understand that the relationship really is over. You may even need time to daydream through a series of "if-only's"—it's natural for someone in your shoes. You may also need to cry a lot. Eventually, you'll be ready to accept what just happened and move on. Here are some ways to deal with your breakup.

Write it out. Pain, numbness, rage, wishful thinking, whatever you're feeling, put it in a poem or a letter to the person you just broke up with. Express it all, and keep in mind that you don't ever have to show it to a soul.

Spend more time kicking it with your crew. You don't have to go through this alone. Tell your friends what you're feeling, so they can help try to cheer you up. Avoid saying things like, "There'll never be another love for me." Instead, remind yourself that someone who deserves you will come along.

Avoid your old hangouts, especially if they just remind you of your ex.

Get active. Do something that helps you let out aggression, like kickboxing, running, or other exercise. Once you start feeling better physically, you'll feel better inside.

Take care of yourself—after all, do you really want to look as bad as you feel? Dress nice, stay clean, try something new with your hair. Then enjoy—and believe—the compliments that come your way.

Find ways to laugh. A good magazine, book, or movie can keep you entertained.

How can i break up gently?

If you're the dumper, not the dumpee, try these suggestions for making a breakup smooth, safe, and as considerate as possible, but real:

✔ Know who you are dealing with and take that into account as you pick a time and place to break the news. Is your partner going to flip out? Pick a public setting or do it by phone. If you're more concerned about your soon-to-be-ex's sadness, then pick a place that will be as comfortable as possible. But don't do it in front of friends—that will just humiliate them.

✔ Try to be honest and kind about why you need to break up. (Be careful if you are breaking off an abusive relationship. See page 53.)

✔ Avoid being cruel or cold about it. Although the news of a breakup is almost never welcome, it's still not right to be mean to someone you once liked or loved, especially if they didn't do you wrong. It's okay though, to say that you need to go for a few weeks or months without seeing each other before you can try to be friends.

> "I caught my boyfriend cheating on me and it hurt so much to let him go. I wanted to give in and take him back but I knew that if he ever played on me again it would only hurt twice as much. But I stayed strong and tried to focus on other things like school, friends, and going out and trying new things as a way to get my mind off of him. Soon I stopped thinking of him as much and I made new friends and had more confidence in myself."
>
> Angelina, 16

> "It was really rough for me to get over my breakup with my ex-boyfriend. We had gone together for so long and I had really deep feelings for him. But when we started having problems he decided it was easier to leave me than to work things out. It was even harder because two days after we broke up I saw him with another girl."
>
> Marie, 17

How do i know if i'm ready for sex?

This is The Big Question. The answer comes down to how you feel and how well you are able to balance your feelings with common sense. Your body and your hormones may be giving you some incredibly strong urges, making the idea of being sexual with someone very tempting.

Don't leave the decision to have sex until the last minute. The best time to think about having sex is not when you're starting to kiss and touch and be "in the moment" with your partner, but when you're alone and able to sort through your thoughts without feeling pressured. Your body is the only one you've got. Does it make sense to share it with the person you're thinking about?

Sex, at its best, is about intimacy. It's about expressing yourself physically and being as close as you can get to someone. If this feels like what you want then it might be time. One group of young women (ages 15 to 18) said the only reason they'd have sex was "to express feelings or love"—especially after going out with somebody for a long time.

If you decide that you want to have sex with your partner, you both owe it to yourselves to be responsible. If your partner is a guy, he's got to wear a condom; if she's a girl, use a Glyde dam or plastic wrap. But if sex right now just doesn't feel right that's reason enough not to do it. Don't sweat it, if that's your gut feeling. Your partner has a right to ask to have sex, and you have a right to say no. Simple as that.

TIPS

Ways to Say No

* "I love you, but I'm just not ready for this now."

* "I don't want you to pressure me to have sex. I'm not ready yet."

* "When we are ready to have sex, it should be special, not some spur-of-the-moment thing."

* "No, I don't want to and I think you should respect my opinion."

* Remember, you can also avoid the question (and having to answer "no") by not being alone with your partner or by having boundaries when you kiss or touch each other when you are alone together.

RELATIONSHIPS

Am I Ready for Sex?

Stuff to Think About

○ Do you know your partner well enough to be very intimate?

○ Does the thought of your partner make you feel good all over?

○ Have you been touching, holding, and kissing each other for a long time and now feel ready to go further?

○ Are you ready to insist that your partner wear a condom to prevent STIs or pregnancy?

○ Are you financially and emotionally stable enough to support a child in case you get pregnant?

○ Do you feel you have something to prove to your friends?

○ Is your partner manipulating you into having sex?

○ Do you trust your partner to respect you or treat you right in the days and weeks after sex?

○ Do you feel that you owe this person sex?

○ Are you expecting sex to be perfect like it is in movies?

○ Which are you more likely to regret later: having sex with this person, or not?

> "It's different for everyone, but I think I started at the right time for me. I thought about it for a long time first. I like having sex, and I'm with someone who cares about me."
> Rachel, 17

> "I have felt strong sexual feelings since I was pretty young. But I know that I'm not ready to have sex yet."
> Joanne, 19

My First Time

by Margarita, 24

My first time with sex was supposed to give me vanity
But I couldn't wait for him to get off of me.

I thought the first time was supposed to be great
But it just felt like a huge mistake.

It was nothing like the stories my friends told me
and nothing like the stuff I see on TV.

No candles, no romance, no sensual feelings.
Just a boy playing me for his sexual healing.

I thought about this night a thousand times in my mind.
But instead of making love I just wasted my time.

Yes, I'm Ready

by Jessica, 16

Yeah I'm ready
matta a fact
I know I'm ready
ready to take this step
this one step I never even thought
I would
or could
but time has proven me wrong
Sex to me is an in the moment thing
You're feelin' like you on one accord with your
partner
heart beating
heavy breathing
and the overwhelming feelin' you needin'
well you know
but just because my body is callin'
Does that mean I'm really ready?
Well you see that's actually only half
the emotions
yeah that's right, my mind must also be ready
sex isn't just a body thing
sometimes we forget
I'm ready, but
I'm not just ready to have sex
I'm ready to protect myself
Ready to understand that sex is not all
a relationship is

"Mostly I enjoy sex on the physical level, but emotionally,
it's a heavy thing. I'm still having problems feeling secure.
I think I started too young."

Jenny, 17

What Is Responsible Sex?

An Interview with Doug, 17

Q: What do you do when you and your girlfriend are going to have sex?
A: Usually she'll bring the condoms since I don't usually carry any on me.

Q: If your partner forgot the condom would you consider unprotected sex?
A: If she forgot to bring the condom we would have unprotected sex. Anyways, we usually have sex without a condom. I don't know why, I guess because in the moment of things you don't want to stop for nothing in the world.

Q: Would you blame it on your girlfriend if you caught a disease?
A: Yes, because I know that I don't have anything.

Q: Since you said that you and your girlfriend sometimes don't use protection, what would you do if she got pregnant?
A: I would take care of my son and make sure he has the Jordans and all the newest shoes.

Q: I noticed you said that you would take care of your son. What about if the child was a girl?
A: I want a boy. I want someone to carry on my name. I don't know what I'd do if it were a girl. I wouldn't be as close to her as I would to him.

I Wasn't Ready

by Lady X, 18

Josiah and I went to the movies. We kissed and touched and basically we really got into the moment. After the show he asked if I would come to his house. I said yes, not thinking about what had just happened in the movies.

At his house, we watched TV for a while. Then we started to kiss. We got into the moment again but this time it was different because we were now alone. Josiah told me to hold on a second and went into his room. When he came back, he immediately sat down and tried to get back into the moment. Soon he started taking off some of my clothes and I started taking off his.

Then he took out a condom. I sat there and watched him put it on, not stopping him. I didn't know how to tell him that I didn't want to have sex because I didn't want to disappoint him. Just as we were about to have sex, I told him that I was not ready. He tried to ignore that I had just told him no.

When he found out I was serious, he flipped on me. He started yelling and told me to get the hell out of his house. A week later, Josiah called and apologized for his actions. He said that I shouldn't lead guys on like that because everybody isn't always going to be as nice as him and I might get raped. But we're still friends and that's cool.

How do i know who my real friends are?

Friends are great to share your feelings with and help you make sense of the world. Friends help you figure out who you are and who you need to be.

Most people find friends through gut instincts and needs. For instance, you may be naturally drawn to someone who is a good listener, or you may feel a need to hang out with someone who has more drama going on in her life than you do. It's possible to pick your friends for the wrong reasons—like how they dress or how popular they are—and later realize you can't really stay friends.

The only way to know who your real friends are is to take the time to get to know them and to pay attention to how you act towards one another through the good times and the bad.

> "I look for honesty, openness, and kind-heartedness in my girlfriends. I know they're my true friends when I talk to them and they won't tell other people what I said. Once one of my friends upset me by putting her boyfriend before me, but I talked it out and let her know how I felt."
>
> Sarah, 17

> "I can't talk to my family that well, but Brian is the one who I talk to about everything. I can just let go with him. The most important trait that he or any good friend could have is being willing to deal with bullshit, being willing to deal with the bad stuff in order to be there for the good stuff."
>
> Alicia, 18

> "Senior year, me and this girl Tiffany used to cut class and go to the Castro and get kumquats and just sit and watch all the gay people because we thought it was great."
>
> Rochelle, 20

Slipping Away

Sometimes you outgrow your friends because your needs change or because newer friends take up more of your time. If you two have had a big blowout, and you know it's over anyway, then maybe it's best to just let it go.

Sometimes friends just start to grow apart, and it's no one's fault. It can be hard to break off a friendship gently. Tell her honestly that you feel like you've grown apart.

Sometimes when a friend moves away it's hard to keep up the friendship on both ends. If phone calls are hard for you to deal with, tell her you're more comfortable writing letters or emails. That way the friendship can survive on a different level. Remember, one day a friend may have to drift away from you, too, so treat old friends like you would want to be treated.

What's a True Friend?

- A friend reads your moods pretty well and checks up on you when something is wrong.
- A friend doesn't judge you too much.
- A friend doesn't flake out on you too often.
- A friend doesn't pressure you to do stuff you don't want to do.
- A friend helps you sort out your problems and doesn't always bring the conversation back to themselves.
- A friend is a good listener.
- A friend may be competitive sometimes, but isn't jealous all the time.
- A friend keeps your secrets and doesn't spread your business all over town.
- A friend is willing to tell you flat out when you're wrong—but not too often.
- A friend isn't friendly only when they want something from you.
- A friend is willing to work through a fight and make up with you when it's over.

How can i get along better with my parents?

It's not always easy to get along with your parents when you're growing up and becoming more independent. You start wanting more privileges, later curfews, more clothes, more music, more phone time, or more time to just kick it with your friends. And maybe your mom or dad wants you to take more responsibility around the house or at school. But at the same time, they may want more control over your life.

If you want to get your parents to lighten up, you need to get to know them well. That way you can imagine what their lives are like. Show your parents that they can appreciate you and trust you—not just because you need something from them—but because you want a better relationship.

Hanging Out with Your Parents

Talk to your parents about your teachers or your schoolwork or your friends, so they'll know more about the pressures you face every day.

Go with them on errands or help them with jobs around the house. This gives you a chance to hang out together.

Ask your parents about their family life when they were your age: their parents, their neighborhood, the chores they used to do, whether they got along with their brothers and sisters, who their favorite relative is or was, what their school cliques were like, their first boyfriend or girlfriend.

Let them know where you're going or what you've been up to as often as possible.

Help around the house before they ask: straighten up the living room, the kitchen table, the bathroom towels, or even surprise them and empty the trash or do the dishes.

If you can tell that your parents are stressed, don't add to it by acting up.

Talking to Parents About the Serious Stuff

Some parents are good listeners and some have no listening skills at all. If this is true for you, it may seem easier to just say, "Forget it. Mom never listens anyway," and keep your feelings to yourself. But sooner or later, you might need the help, connections, and advice of an adult in your house before you make your next move.

> "Even though Mom always complains about me being such a disobedient teenager, she does care about me in her way. I'm learning to ignore her words and concentrate on the small things she does. I don't take them for granted."
>
> Wanda, 16

TIPS
Talking with Your Parents

✽ Pick a time when your or mom or dad is in a pretty good mood and alone.

✽ Give signals or cues that show you mean business. Try, "Ma, I have something really, really serious to tell you." The goal here is not about acting up, but getting your parent's attention and keeping it.

✽ Don't try to demand that your parent is sworn to secrecy. Depending on the issue, this may be a promise that a parent can't—or shouldn't—keep.

✽ Think about what you want from them in advance. Is it realistic? Is it fair? Maybe they'll have another solution that you hadn't thought of.

✽ Try asking them if they ever had to face your situation when they were a teenager.

✽ Have faith—even strict parents can tell when it's time to think before they act. If you have your doubts, say: "I need you to first think about this before you do anything."

✽ If your mom or dad starts accusing you in the middle of your talk, don't let it escalate by yelling back. Try to stay calm and remind them that you need their help, not their criticism.

How can i stay strong and safe in my family?

If you're lucky, your family's a safe place for you. It's where you go to find sanity, support, and comfort. A family also shares some basic opinions about the difference between right and wrong. Of course, everyone doesn't always agree, but in a family like this, there's a general sense that, "Hey, we can handle this together."

This sounds good on paper, but not every family has issues that can easily be let go. On the real side, some families feel like a war zone, with family members endlessly fighting and bitching and tripping about one thing or another. Others feel like the Twilight Zone, with everyone walking around and not seeming to notice that there is some seriously wrong and harmful stuff going down.

If you are in a difficult family situation, you'll need to learn how to get the aid, support—and in some cases—intervention that you need to stay in one piece. If you are experiencing abuse in your family, or if you have been witnessing the abuse of a family member, it's easy to feel isolated and to think that this only happens in your family. Child abuse, neglect, and domestic violence are far more common than some people admit, and there are 24-hour hotlines that can help.

There are some family situations that you can live with. Other situations are dangerous, and you need to get outside help. Below are two lists of situations that will help you distinguish between situations you have to put up with and the ones you don't.

In many families, there's a spoken or unspoken code that says the stuff that goes on behind closed doors should stay in the family and is nobody else's business. But if there is abuse going on in your home, it's a serious issue and it's important to put a stop to it—not just for yourself, but for your other siblings, too.

Where can i get help?

First try going to relatives you can trust; they may be able to have you come live with them until things get better at home. Otherwise, talk to your teacher, school counselor, or principal. Call 411 to get the number for **Child Protective Services** in your county, and call them to report child abuse in your home. If there's a fight going on, call the police rather than getting involved yourself.

HOTLINE

24-Hour Hotlines

National Domestic Violence/Abuse Hotline
1-800-799-SAFE (7233)

RAINN: Rape, Abuse, Incest National Network
1-800-656-HOPE (4673)

Child Help USA/National Child Abuse Hotline
1-800-4-A-CHILD (422-4453)

Family Problems You Gotta Get Help With

☆ parents neglecting or ignoring children

☆ parents or children drinking excessively or taking drugs

☆ physical abuse like hitting, slapping, beating, arm twisting, or pulling hair

☆ frequent threats of violence towards a child or another family member

☆ frequent cursing, yelling, humiliating, or otherwise verbally abusing a family member

☆ parents or siblings making sexual suggestions or comments

☆ parents or siblings touching the breasts, genitals, or buttocks, or any other body part of another family member in a suggestive or seductive way or demanding intercourse or oral sex

Family Problems You May Have to Accept

☆ parents who have new relationships after divorce or death in the family

☆ occasional battles between siblings

☆ parents yelling sometimes

☆ friction based on personality differences

☆ disagreements about having to obey a stepparent or a parent's boyfriend or girlfriend

FACTS

✳ Of all rapes and sexual assaults, 75% involve family members, relatives, or acquaintances; 22% involve strangers; and 3% have an uncertain or undetermined relationship.

✳ Girls are sexually abused almost three times more often than boys.

Source: Pacific Center for Violence Prevention

Taking Care of Yourself

Speak up for yourself firmly and respectfully. Show your family that you are growing older now and have different needs now (more privacy, more freedom, more respect, acknowledgment that you are maturing).

Set boundaries. These will be different in each family. In some families you might need to insist that other members respect your privacy when your door is closed. In another family, you might request that you not be expected to take the responsibilities and workload of an adult.

Find ways to declare truce when you've had a fight: a little note, a small gift, a gesture, or a compliment—something that suggests you want things to be cool again.

Make sure that you always have an adult (or super-responsible, resourceful friend) whom you can go to if things get unbearable at home.

How to Build a Safety Net

Adapted from Karen DeBord at the University of Missouri-Columbia

1. Take a blank sheet of paper and draw a circle in the middle. That represents you.

2. Around that first circle, write all the names of family members, friends, or acquaintances that you're in contact with. Circle their names.

3. Draw a solid line between your name and those people whom you can always count on for support.

4. Put dotted lines between your name and the people you can sometimes count on for support.

5. On the outer corners of your "net," jot down all the places you feel safe—whether it's home or the local library. Draw a box or the symbol for a house around these places.

6. Now think of the people in your life who you cannot count on for support. What places in your life are dangerous?

Are there ways that you can build stronger relationships with some of the reliable people in your net? Do you need a wider net? What do you have to do to be able to draw more solid lines? Do you have at least two safe houses? How can you avoid people and places that make you feel unsafe?

Having Somewhere to Go Kept Me Going
by Cynthia, 16

The year I turned 11, Daddy got remarried. My brother and I had one good year before things went downhill. Then my stepmother started beating me, taunting me, and otherwise making my life miserable. She would get in my face and snarl mean things and I could see globs of spit at the corners of her mouth. Or she would beat me with her fists or a brush and break my glasses or pull my hair. Sometimes Dad was home to see this. Often he looked the other way.

But my Aunt Sonia (who was really just a family friend) could tell that something bad was going on when she visited us. So she would take me and my brother out to the park or to the movies. One day Aunt Sonia took me aside and gave me a piece of paper with her phone number on it. If I ever needed to run away, she told me, I could come stay with her. I thought of taking her up on that many times, but I was worried that sooner or later she'd have to send me home and there'd be hell to pay.

Luckily, my father and stepmother soon had sense enough to send me down South to my Aunt Ivy's for the summer. Staying in a new home for six weeks was the bomb and that helped cool things off at home a lot. Aunt Ivy also made an offer like Sonia's to me. Just knowing that Aunt Sonia and Aunt Ivy were there for me is what helped me get through the next year.

How do i look out for myself?

"Think of yourself as holding a safety shield," says Lori Dobeus, the director of the San Francisco Women's Safety Project. There are five parts to this shield:

1 *Prevention.* Always have a healthy awareness of your surroundings.

2 *Avoidance.* Stay away from situations that put you at risk.

3 *Confrontation.* Use your voice to stand up for yourself and to defend yourself physically.

4 *After Care.* Get help for your body and spirit if you've been the victim of an attack.

5 *Organizing.* Take self-defense, teach it to others, volunteer at a crisis center, or work to make your neighborhood safe.

When you think about safety issues, think about the first two parts of this shield: prevention and avoidance. "But it's a myth that if you practice prevention, you'll never be victimized," says Lori. "You need to work on all of these areas; otherwise, there's a hole in your shield."

Safety is not about living in fear or restricting your movements. It's about knowing what you'll do if something happens. But most situations are unique and complicated: what works in one instance or for one person might not work for you. With that in mind, here are some ways to take care of yourself.

Prevention & Avoidance

Trust Your Instincts

Ever have the feeling that something's wrong? You don't know what, but you just know it. Trust this feeling. If you're uncomfortable in a situation or feel you might be in danger, it's okay to act on it. Don't worry about being rude or embarrassed. Get somewhere you feel safe. Your power comes from trusting these inner warnings.

Date Safety

✔ **Use the buddy system** where you pair up with a friend to keep track of each other. When you first go out with someone, it's smart to double date or go out with a group.

✔ **Tell a friend where you're going** and when you expect to be back. You can even check in with your friend and let her know how things are going during the date.

✔ **Don't let your date make all the decisions.** Have some input into the plans.

✔ **Speak up if you're uncomfortable** at any point. Say what you really want and what you're feeling. If your date doesn't hear you or respect your wishes, this gives you a lot of information about that person.

✔ **Meet somewhere public.** Bring enough bus fare so you won't have to depend on your date for transportation. Also, it's not a good idea to leave a group scene or get a ride home from someone you don't know that well.

✔ **Remember that alcohol and drugs** can interfere with your judgment and put you more at risk. So be prepared if you think you're going to drink.

✔ **Set sexual limits** and communicate them. Tell your partner when to STOP if you're not comfortable with something. Don't be afraid of offending them.

✔ **If you're uncomfortable with the date at any point, end it.** Say you have to leave, you're sick, whatever.

Confrontation

You're hanging with your friends. Maybe you're on the street, at school, or at a park. Other groups of people are kicking it too. Then someone insults you, starts to pick a fight. This may be one of those times when it's better to protect your body and sacrifice your pride. You can respond and risk a fight. Or you can ignore it. Walk away. Don't engage. Sometimes exiting from a situation is your best defense.

What Can I Do if I'm Attacked?

Remember that there is no one right thing to do. Studies have shown that women who resist a sexual assault are more likely to escape than women who don't. If there are multiple attackers, running is your best defense. It's hard to reason or fight back if there's more than one person.

Sometimes, a combination of strategies works. Here are some ways to fight an attacker:

✔ **Yell and make as much noise as possible.**

✔ **Try to reason with your attacker:** Talk him out of it; tell him that what he's doing hurts you; ask him to stop.

✔ **Use a weapon**—a key, pencil, anything you have—but if you decide to do this, make sure you follow through 100%. The weapon could end up being used against you.

Some suggest carrying mace or pepper spray. Unfortunately, both could misfire and wind up in your eyes. If you carry a spray, be prepared for this possibility. And once you start to use a weapon on someone, follow through. This will lessen the risk of the weapon being turned onto you.

If you fight back against your attacker, go for these primary target areas where a person is most vulnerable. Poke or hit hard in their eyes, nose, throat, groin, knees, and collarbone.

Sometimes talking to your attacker could get you out of a sexual assault. Say anything you can think of, try to relate as a person if you think this would do any good. Or you might say you're pregnant, or that you have an STI. Or cry hysterically or pee or vomit—something to throw the attacker off-guard. No one thing works in all situations, so just try to gather your thoughts and see what might work.

If you're afraid to fight back, don't. If you think that giving in to a sexual attack is the best method for staying alive, then it is. Your main priority is surviving, and if keeping silent and doing what the attacker says will help you get to the other side, then it's the right strategy.

After Care

If you have been attacked, remember:

✔ **Don't blame yourself;** your attacker committed the crime, not you.

✔ **Try not to feel guilty;** you didn't do anything wrong.

✔ **Get help;** you don't have to suffer in silence. Find a support group, call a hotline, and talk to friends or a supportive parent if you have one. You can also file a report with the police. Their job is to help you by finding the attacker and keeping him off the streets.

Organizing

Take a self-defense course. Local rape crisis centers usually offer or know good classes in martial arts and self-defense. Some high schools and many colleges also offer free self-defense workshops. Once you've taken a course yourself, if you liked it, you can spread the word to your friends.

Help make your neighborhood safer by volunteering or working with a community-based organization that works for social change.

Keeping yourself safe is really about being aware of yourself in the world: knowing when you're taking risks, assessing the danger of situations, and preparing what you might do if something happens.

Watch Your Back

On the Street

Walk fast and look like you know where you are going, even if you don't. Walk facing traffic and make sure you're out where it's well lit. If you think someone is following you, cross the street and walk faster. Go to a store or a place where there are other people. If it's an emergency, break a fire alarm (those boxes you see on the street) and pull it or break a window. The fire department will get there fast, maybe even faster than the police will. And you can always shout "fire." Yelling alone could scare off a would-be attacker.

At Home

You are more likely to be in danger from sexual assault in your own home than you are on the street. Statistics show that rape and sexual assault most often occur between people you know: dates, boyfriends, ex's, acquaintances. Knowing this is one way to prevent sexual assault. If you or someone you know has been sexually assaulted, see Hotlines on page 60.

Online

Online chatting can be a lot of fun, but be aware that the person you are chatting with might be lying about who or what they are. People may represent themselves as younger or older than they actually are; males may log on with a female name and vice versa. You should always remain anonymous when in chat rooms—make up a cool, gender-neutral screen name—and never give out private information about yourself, including where you live, your phone number, or where you go to school. It can be dangerous to set up a face-to-face meeting with someone you've met online. If you choose to do so, meet in a public place and let someone know where you're going to be. If someone you're chatting with makes you feel uncomfortable in any way, quickly sign off.

What is rape?

Rape is a crime of violence and power! Sex is the weapon—not the cause. You don't "deserve" it no matter how you dress or act.

What is acquaintance rape?

It could be your first date. Or maybe you've been seeing the guy for a few months now. Or you're just out with some of your closest guy pals. You're at a party and you're drinking. You start kissing and one thing leads to another and you're alone with a cute boy and you're naked. At first you want to have sex. You say yes. Then you change your mind and say no. You want him to stop, but he doesn't. You push him away. He pushes you back. He forces you down. He tells you that you want it. You don't. You said no. But you feel like it's your fault because you led him to think it. Is this rape? Yes. It's called date or acquaintance rape. There usually aren't any bruises or witnesses. Often it's a case of what he said vs. what she said. And many times, the guy doesn't even realize that what he did was rape. But sex without your consent is not sex. It's violence. And it's a crime.

If you are under the influence of drugs or alcohol, you are considered legally unable to give your consent to sex. If someone forces you to have sex, it is rape, especially if you were drunk.

What is statutory rape?

As far as the law goes, having sexual intercourse with a minor (17 years of age or under) is statutory rape. The law says that minors, just because of their age, are not able to say yes to sex. The law was originally designed to protect young people from older people who could take advantage of them.

Each state decides the age when a person can say yes to sexual activity. This is the age of consent. In California, both you and your boyfriend have to be at least 18 to be able to have sex legally. So technically, both of you could be charged with statutory rape. You probably wouldn't be, though, because someone has to want to press charges (like your parents), and even if they do, statutory rape between consenting minors usually isn't prosecuted.

For comparison, Alaska and New Jersey make the age of consent 16, Colorado and New York say 17, and Tennessee says 18. The age of consent laws keep changing. Check out www.ageofconsent.com for the latest updates for all 50 states. Remember, the age of consent is an arbitrary age created by lawmakers. It doesn't mean you are or aren't ready to have sex. That's a decision only you can make for yourself.

QUIZ

Test Your Knowledge

1. If a young woman wears sexy clothing, it's her fault if she gets raped. **TRUE / FALSE**

2. Your husband or boyfriend can't rape you if you had sex with him before. **TRUE / FALSE**

3. If you're drunk and forced to have sex with someone, it's rape. **TRUE / FALSE**

4. Rape cannot happen between two members of the same sex. **TRUE / FALSE**

5. People only get raped at night. **TRUE / FALSE**

6. When a person gets raped, the first thing to do is take a shower and call for help. **TRUE / FALSE**

7. People who get raped usually know their rapist. **TRUE / FALSE**

8. A young woman can always tell if she is raped. **TRUE / FALSE**

9. It's okay for a guy to force a young woman to have sex if he spent money on a date. **TRUE / FALSE**

10. If you're 16 years old and your boyfriend is 18, it's legal for you to have sex with him. **TRUE / FALSE**

Answers:
1. False. 2. False. 3. True. 4. False. 5. False. 6. False. 7. True. 8. False. 9. False 10. True/False

FACTS

✳ About three quarters of all rapes occur between people who know each other.

✳ Most rapes happen between 6 PM and 6 AM, but rape can occur anytime, anywhere.

✳ Teens aged 16 to 19 are twice as likely to be victims of rape and assault than women in any other age group.

✳ A woman is raped or sexually assaulted every eight minutes somewhere in the United States.

✳ Less than one in three rapes is reported. Women say they don't report it because they're ashamed or they fear their attacker will get back at them.

RIGHTS

What do i do if i've been raped?

> "When somebody rapes you, they're taking away your civil and human rights. They're making you do something with your body you don't want to do. They're dehumanizing you."
>
> Jamie, Rape Crisis Counselor,
> San Francisco Women Against Rape (SFWAR)

How to Deal Emotionally with Rape
by Wanda and Stephanie

It's bad enough that rape messes you up physically for awhile. The mental and emotional effects of rape are a whole different thing. If you've been raped, you might experience a kind of emotional shock called post-traumatic stress disorder. This is the same syndrome that people who have lived through a war or natural disaster might feel. And nobody, but nobody, should have to go through it alone.

You may have any of the following: nightmares, flashbacks, depression, numbness, denial, fear that you'll be raped again, inability to trust or love anyone, and the feeling that the rape was your fault. This business of blaming yourself for the rape is so hard to shake. But you gotta try: No matter how you acted or what you wore or what you said, rape is rape. It was not your fault. Whatever you did during the assault, it was right—because you are alive.

If you're like other people who've been raped, you may also feel like a part of you has died. Perhaps a part of you did die. But a rape survivor needs to also think about the part of her that's alive, the part that's struggling to come out wiser and stronger and whole again. That's why you shouldn't go through this alone. If you can't bring yourself to call a therapist or rape counselor, have a friend or teacher or one of your parents—someone you know will help you—call for you. Not every therapist is good at handling post-traumatic stress disorder, so find someone who specializes in rape counseling. Know that you don't have to get over the rape in any particular time frame. Go easy on yourself. It may take a whole lot of time to heal wounds this deep.

HOTLINE
24-Hour Hotlines
RAINN: Rape, Abuse, Incest National Network
1-800-656-HOPE (4673)

Child Help USA/National Child Abuse Hotline
1-800-4-A-CHILD (422-4453)

If You've Been Raped

Rape can be a brutal experience. But if you've survived a rape or sexual assault, there are people you can call and things you can do to help with your recovery. If you've been raped:

Don't wash yourself. You may desperately want to wash yourself or change your clothes, but don't. Your body and clothing can be used as evidence.

Call someone you care about and tell them. You can also call the free national rape crisis hotline 24 hours a day or a local rape crisis center. If you're under 18, you might not want to mention your age when you call. By law, some hotlines may be required to report the rape of a minor. You also don't have to give your name if you don't want to, so you can talk to a counselor in complete confidence. It may be hard to talk to a stranger about what happened, but these centers are staffed with people who understand what you might be going through and they are trained to help.

Get medical help. If you go to a rape crisis center, a staff member can go with you to the hospital or clinic. If you've changed, bring the clothing that you were wearing at the time of the assault. If you haven't changed, bring another set of clothing for after the exam. At the hospital, you'll be examined for injuries and bruises. You'll also be offered what is called a "rape kit." The provider will examine you and collect and label evidence of the assault. The provider may photograph any cuts, bruises, or scratches; take saliva samples; clean your fingernails for evidence; search for semen stains or hair in your underpants; or conduct a pelvic exam. It sounds like a lot, but gathering this information can be a powerful tool if you decide you want to prosecute. If you're not sure, you're best off getting the rape kit done just in case you decide to prosecute later.

The doctor or nurse will also discuss treatment for the prevention of STIs and pregnancy, emergency contraception, and information about HIV/AIDS. If you're under 18, the healthcare provider is legally required to notify your parents.

You can go to the police. Reporting the rape to the police is up to you, but the best time to do it is soon after the incident. You can ask for a woman officer to talk to, if you like. Reporting does not mean pressing charges and taking your rapist to court. But it can help the police investigate, and your information may help solve other rape cases.

You can always decide not to bring charges after you report, but telling your story to the police may help you heal. Although it may be painful to tell the details again to an officer, you may feel you're getting back some of your control and power by not keeping silent. It's helpful to have a friend or family member with you. A staff member from the rape crisis center could also meet you at the police station.

What do i do if i'm kicked out?

Your parents can't really kick you out—or they're not supposed to. Legally, they're your guardians.

But sometimes young people run away because the situation at home has gotten so bad. If you or a friend find yourself on the street, here are some ways to get help.

✔ Call a friend to let someone know what's happening.

✔ If you can, stay at an adult friend's house or a friend's place with her parent's permission.

✔ Call the National Runaway Switchboard (1-800-621-4000) anytime, 24 hours a day. Or call a youth crisis line where you live. These hotlines can lead you to nearby shelters, help with transportation home, or give messages to your family.

✔ If you feel you're in danger, call the police. The most important thing is to get someplace safe. The streets are not safe.

Most youth crisis centers can offer you a place to stay for a few days while you get help working things out. You would meet with an intake counselor and answer some questions about what's going on in your life. The counselor will contact your family and ask them some questions about the situation at home. Often the shelter will offer family mediation or therapy in order to find ways to help you and your family work things out and communicate better.

What is emancipation?

Emancipation is a legal process that allows minors as young as 14 and up to 18 to be free of their parents' care and custody. You can get emancipation by petitioning the court. You have to convince the court that you're willing and able to live apart from your parents or guardians, that you can support yourself and manage your finances, and that emancipation is in your own best interest.

The good thing about emancipation is that you get to make decisions about your life yourself. You can apply for a work permit, enroll yourself in school, get a bank loan or a credit card. By emancipating yourself, though, you no longer have the right to be supported by your parents or guardians. You have to support yourself financially, even though you may still be restricted from working certain jobs or hours.

> "I used to run away for weeks. I was so depressed and frustrated with myself. I had no friends. I felt worthless and ugly. I felt like I didn't deserve to live. I had nobody to talk to, so the best thing for me was to leave."
>
> **Anonymous**

FACTS

* More young women than men run away or leave their homes.
* Most young women are eventually reunited with their families.
* There are over 1.3 million young people living on the streets in the United States.

24-Hour Hotlines

California Youth Crisis Line 1-800-843-5200
Confidential crisis counseling and referrals to shelter for at risk and homeless youth.

National Runaway Switchboard 1-800-621-4000
24 hours a day counseling and referrals.

What should i think about before running away?

> "I ran away a couple of times because there was too much drama happening at home. Every day felt like I was at war. My mom and her boyfriend would fight about little things. And whatever I was doing, I was always in trouble. I get good grades. I don't even cut school. I think my mom's boyfriend brainwashed her. She's changed, and so have I."
>
> Francis, 16

THINK

Before you run away, ask yourself . . .

* Is there anything else I can do to improve my situation?
* Do I have somewhere safe to go?
* Who can I call to help me?
* How will I survive?
* What do I want to change by running away?

> "I used to run away to be with my boyfriend. My mom hated him and didn't let him visit or call. I loved him because he was the only one that understood me. Until he dumped me. I realized I was stupid for running away. I realized my mom was right, he was a jerk!"
>
> Cindy, 18

Interview with Bill from Huckleberry House, a San Francisco youth crisis shelter

by Diane, 15

Q: What are the results of running away?
A: When you run away, you think about things like: Where am I gonna stay? Where am I gonna take a shower? Where am I gonna get clean clothes to wear? Even if you run to a friend's house, you're not gonna be able to stay there forever. You really have to think about what you're going to do to keep yourself safe.

Q: Where can you go if you run away?
A: It depends. If you're getting abused, any teacher or trusted adult should help you find a safe place to stay. Most towns have temporary shelters for youths who are being abused. If you're running away because you don't like your parents' rules, then you have fewer options. Try calling your local shelter to see if they'll let you stay there for awhile.

Q: What's the longest you can stay?
A: It depends on the rules of the shelter. At Huckleberry House, if your parents don't do anything about the situation, you can stay as long as you want. If your parents report you to the police as a runaway or a missing person, then they find out you're at the shelter, they have the right to say, "You don't have permission to stay. You have to come home now."

Q: Do shelters have curfews?
A: Every shelter is different. When you're staying at Huckleberry House, you're expected to go to school. We don't really have a curfew because if you're not at school, you have to be here. There's a bus that takes young people back and forth on weekdays.

Q: Can you get in trouble if you shelter a runaway?
A: You can't offer an underage person shelter without the parent's permission. Of course, you could offer them a place to stay if they feel unsafe or need a place for a short while because this law is hardly ever prosecuted. At Huckleberry House, we can shelter young people because there's a section of the law that says if you're over 12, you have the right to consent to your own services.

Q: What happens if you run away because you've been abused?
A: It's actually good for a young person to run away if it's unsafe at home. Once you're in a shelter, you'd tell a staff person why you ran away. That person makes a report to the department of social services (DSS), who will start an investigation. It's their job to decide if your home is a safe place or not. They try their best to keep families together, and if you're sent back home, they try to help out with counseling and problem solving. If they don't find your home to be safe for you, they can put you in a foster home, or try to find another person in your family who you can stay with.

Q: What are ways to make money if you run away?
A: The same ways anyone makes money, except if you're underage, you need a work permit that has to be signed by your parents. Some youth panhandle or sell drugs. Not everyone who runs away becomes a prostitute. But getting money is not that easy when you don't have a place to stay.

Q: What happens if I get kicked out often?
A: You need to think about why you're getting kicked out to see if there's behavior that can change. Ask for help to try and get another perspective on the situation that may help change things for the better.

What are my rights at school?

Most school handbooks say that if you get caught bringing drugs or alcohol to campus, you can get suspended from school sometimes for five days. In some states, you may even get expelled. If you cut too many classes, you may be considered truant and you could get arrested.

Of course, not everyone who drinks or does drugs or cuts school gets caught, but if you're doing these things regularly, it may be a sign that something else is going on. What's really happening?

- ✔ Are you unhappy with a teacher? Or with the administration?
- ✔ Are the classes too difficult or not challenging enough?
- ✔ Do you fit in with your classmates and do you like them?
- ✔ Is there anything at home that makes you feel like not going to school?

Talk these things over with a counselor or call a youth line or community center—look in your local phone book or check the numbers listed in the resource section of this book. Check out if your school has a good peer-counseling program. Together, you may be able to find alternative solutions, like if you're cutting English every day because you hate it, you could see if you can take an independent study instead.

Can i wear whatever i want to school?

Most schools allow you to wear clothing or accessories like buttons, scarves, and armbands that express your feelings and beliefs. But all schools have the right to decide if your clothing or hairstyle interferes with your learning or is unsafe in any way. For instance, some school authorities argue that wearing certain clothing or colors is a sign of gang affiliation. Or T-shirts that promote guns and violence could be considered unsafe to other students. The school could prohibit such clothing in order to protect all the students and/or prevent substantial disruption and interference in learning.

Staying in School

by Isabel, 18

When I was a sophomore, I hated myself. I was lonely and felt extremely ugly, from the inside out. I never liked school. I would show up for a day or two each week just to keep them off my back.

My friends and I would cut school and go to the mall and steal clothes, music, makeup, whatever. Or we would drink or do any drugs we could get. I tried speed, weed, even chemo. It was fun to experiment—I definitely liked some drugs better than others.

Three months passed and I stopped going to school. Then one day, when I came home from wandering around, my mom was on my bed waiting for me with a note. It was a truancy letter saying I would go to juvenile hall if I didn't show up to school.

My mom cried and asked me why. I said stupidly, "I don't know." So the next day I was dragged to school. I couldn't stand being there. I felt like I was suffocating. I couldn't be three minutes late to class or I would get a speech from my teacher, my counselor, and my mom. I was monitored all the time.

I had no choice. I was there, so I decided to do my work. Over time I made friends; my self-image changed. I still hate school, but I want to graduate so I can get out and do the things I want to.

"Me and my friends decided to get drunk one day at school. So we went to a store around 10 AM to steal alcohol, then we went to a laundromat a block away. We finished the bottle. As I was throwing it away, they started smoking weed and I took a hit. I was really messed up. I was so messed up that I only remember walking through the laundromat and that's about it. Everything else blacked out. I woke up in the middle of the night, went to the bathroom, and threw up. I woke my brother up because I was desperate to know what happened. My brother told me that I went back to school and it was obvious that I was trashed. I got suspended for five days, and had a parent conference scheduled for the end of the week."

Diane, 15

RIGHTS

What are my rights with the police?

Y ou've probably seen this scene on TV a hundred times: Someone is arrested, the police handcuff them, then read the person their rights. There's a bit of mumbling and then it's off to the station house.

Ever wonder what those rights are? You and everyone else in the United States are protected by the Miranda Warning, which goes like this:

"You have the right to remain silent. Anything you say can and will be used against you in a court of law. You have the right to speak to an attorney, and to have an attorney present during any questioning. If you cannot afford a lawyer, one will be provided for you at government expense."

Can the police question me without reading me the Miranda Warning?

Yes. They can ask you your name, address, date of birth, and social security number to establish your identity. Although you have the right under the Miranda Warning not to say anything to the police without an attorney, it probably would help you to cooperate with them by giving this basic information about you.

The police can question you anywhere—at the principal's office, at home, on the street. You always have the right to not say anything, even if your parents are there. And remember that anything you say can be used by the police against you in a court of law.

If you feel your rights have been violated or that you've been mistreated, file a written complaint with the department's internal affairs division or civilian complaint board. The receptionist at the police station should know where to direct you if you ask.

Can the police search my book bag or purse on the street? Can they search my locker at school?

In most states, the police have the right to search a locker at any time because the locker is school property. Some states have decided that the police can only search a locker when they have good reason to believe that the locker holds something illegal.

But the police cannot search you or your book bag without "reasonable suspicion" that you did something wrong or have something illegal in your possession. A police officer may ask to search your book bag or purse, but you don't have to agree.

TIPS

What to Do if You're Stopped by the Police

* Be polite and respectful. Don't badmouth the officer, even if they're being stupid or disrespectful to you. If you're nasty, it could give them reason to arrest you.

* Stay calm and in control of your emotions, body language, and words because anything could be misinterpreted later.

* Keep your hands where the police can see them.

* Don't run. Don't resist, even if you believe you're innocent.

* Don't touch any police officer.

* Don't complain on the scene; don't tell the police they're wrong, or that you're going to file a complaint.

* Don't make statements regarding what happened.

* Ask for a lawyer immediately.

* Remember the officers' badge and patrol car numbers.

* Write down everything you remember as soon as possible.

Source: The American Civil Liberties Union's "Bust Card"

Caught Shoplifting
by Nana, 15

Well one time I got caught shoplifting—I was stealing a pair of $55 pants for my dad for Fathers' Day while carrying a half-full bottle of brandy in my purse. Right after I got caught, they told me to fill out some forms with all this information. They said if I lied, I'd get in more trouble. And they said they had to talk to my parents.

The cop who arrested me called my mom, and with my bad luck, my older cousin who speaks both English and Spanish translated what the cop was saying. I had to go to Juvenile Hall to get my fingerprints and picture taken. I also had paperwork that said I couldn't go back to the store until I was 18.

When I got to the police station, my cousin, her husband, and my mom were there. My mom was crying a lot. My cousin's husband was telling me not to trip because he's been through worse, but that what I did was really surprising coming from me.

They gave me a ticket and told me I had to go to a thief awareness class. I went. They just gave us packets of information and we watched a movie about shoplifting and how everyone sees you.

Do i have the freedom to write or say anything?

The First Amendment: Freedom of Speech

Your right to speak your mind or write what you want is protected by law in the U.S. Constitution, particularly in the amendments called the Bill of Rights. These laws guarantee certain fundamental rights—freedom of religion, freedom of speech and the press, and freedom to assemble, to gather together in groups and take part in rallies and demonstrations. Here's what the amendment actually says about freedom of expression:

"Congress shall make no law . . . prohibiting the free exercise thereof; or abridging the freedom of speech, or of the press." However, just because we are legally free to write and speak our minds, doesn't mean that it always happens.

QUIZ

Do You Feel Free to Express Yourself?

1. Do you watch what you say in front of certain adults, like parents or teachers?

   Almost never / Sometimes / Most of the time / All of the time

2. Are you afraid to write what you think because of what someone else might say?

   Almost never / Sometimes / Most of the time / All of the time

3. Do you limit your language and then have a hard time putting your thoughts into words?

   Almost never / Sometimes / Most of the time / All of the time

4. Would you speak out if you were being treated unfairly?

   Almost never / Sometimes / Most of the time / All of the time

5. Do you speak up for other people when you see them getting pushed around?

   Almost never / Sometimes / Most of the time / All of the time

Answers: If your answers were mostly "Most of the time" or "All of the time," you probably have no problem speaking up. If you circled mostly "Sometimes" and "Almost never," you may be censoring yourself—putting limits around your expression. Are you afraid of what might happen if you said or wrote what you really thought?

What the Law Says

Your right to express your opinions doesn't end when you go to school. However, schools can put certain restrictions around freedom of expression. If school officials find that what you're doing—handing out leaflets or protesting on the school steps, for example—"materially and substantially" disrupts classes and learning, they can ask you to stop. It doesn't sound like the young woman distributing flyers during passing period was disrupting classes (see next page), so she was probably within her rights. Yet if the case was taken to court, and if the school proved that her passing out flyers interfered with learning, the school would probably win.

Can we write whatever we want in the school newspaper?

It depends. If the newspaper is an official school publication, meaning the school pays for it, public school administrators can censor articles they think are "inappropriate" or "harmful." If the paper is entirely student run and paid for, the school cannot put restrictions on the articles nor prevent you from handing it out at school—as long as it doesn't materially and substantially disrupt school activities. Check with your local chapter of the American Civil Liberties Union (ACLU) to see what the laws are in your state. Many states, like California, give students more freedom of speech rights than the Bill of Rights itself.

Do I have to say the Pledge of Allegiance at school?

Not if you don't want to. Making you say anything violates your First Amendment rights. If you prefer, it's fine to remain silent.

Does my school have the right to ban certain books?

This issue continues to create controversy. Censorship is illegal, and schools can't reject books just because they don't agree with authors' viewpoints. However, schools can choose the books they think have the greatest educational value, so they may use this argument for choosing some authors over others.

Knowing your civil liberties and how the Bill of Rights applies to your everyday life can help you be stronger, braver, and more confident. The freedom to read, think, and say what you want are rights worth fighting for.

Young Women Speak Up!

"One day in class I was sitting quiet, as usual. A substitute teacher was yapping away about his boring life. Some students were talking out loud and the teacher got mad. He walked towards the blackboard yelling to us, 'You guys don't even know how behind you are and you're in class yapping, wasting time, when you can be listening to me.' My friend said, 'Well, we're talking cause all you do is talk about your life that we already heard.'

The teacher got madder and started to draw a line on the blackboard. 'All of you are here,' he said. 'And these other kids are way ahead of you, here. And this is the finish line.'

I got mad and said, 'You don't even know us so don't be comparing me with other people I don't know.' Then I asked what school these other people go to. He said, 'A better one than this one.' And I said, 'Why are you comparing us to people in a better school? Compare us to a school just like this one and then maybe I'll agree.'

A couple of minutes passed by and Janet, the secretary, came in to take roll. The teacher told Janet about my friend and said, 'I want him out of here.' I started defending my friend and said, 'Well, you shouldn't have compared us to other people.' Immediately the teacher said, 'I want her out of here too. She's got an attitude problem.' So I walked out. I don't like that teacher since that incident."

"I started to pass my flyers around at school, during passing period. Then the security guard told me that the principal wanted to talk to me. I went down to the office and the principal told me that I couldn't pass my flyers around because I was supporting communism. He also said it was against the law. I told him that those were my ideas and that I was not supporting communism. Then he argued back that I was interfering with other students' educational time. That really pissed me off because I was passing my flyers out during passing period. I thought we had freedom of the press. I guess not because somehow someone always has control over you. I think it's unfair."

"My counselor was deciding to put me in an English class that I already passed. I heard her tell this to a teacher. (Yes, I was eavesdropping.) I went in there and told them I did not need that class. I already passed it and I wasn't about to waste my time. They were surprised. She listened to me. I felt pretty good."

"One time when a store clerk wouldn't help me, I told the manager."

"I felt very sad for almost a month because someone always asked me to have sex with him. I felt very scared and I didn't know what to do, so I cut school and cried. My friends supported me, and then I stood up for myself. I said no to him and continued going to school and studying hard."

"When someone was making fun of me, I yelled at her and told her to stop. They never bothered me again."

"The school district is planning to give my school a grant. We'd get a full-time nurse and more funding for the arts. The bad thing is that a cop would be hired also. I personally wouldn't like a cop harassing me at school. So I decided to write my opinion on paper. I'm also against Proposition 21 so I wrote about that too."

"A guy touched my ass on the bus. I pushed him almost off the stairs and started yelling at him and I made him apologize."

71

What is sexual harassment?

Flirting is fun. It feels good. Sexual harassment doesn't. And that's the big difference. If you repeatedly get sexual comments or attention that you don't want, and that make you feel uncomfortable, then it's not fun—it's sexual harassment. Often this happens when one person has more power over another and uses this power in an abusive way. Sexual harassment is about power and control.

The law recognizes sexual harassment through the eyes of the person receiving the harassment. If you decide the repeated verbal or physical sexual conduct is unwelcome, it's harassment. If you think you're being harassed, ask yourself how the behavior makes you feel. If you're embarrassed, upset, or uncomfortable, and if the sexual actions or comments are repeated, it may be harassment.

Sexual harassment is against the law. Many states, like California, have sexual harassment policies in schools to protect your rights. Some young women have sued their school or work over sexual harassment. If you experience sexual harassment at school or work, first tell the harasser to stop, and then report it to an official or your boss. If the behavior doesn't stop or if you want to take legal action, you can report it to the Office of Civil Rights (OCR), the federal agency created to punish these types of violations. You have 180 days from the date of the incident to file a report.

Test Your Knowledge

Is this sexual harassment?

1. A person makes a sexist joke in front of you.

2. A teacher says he will give you a good grade if you let him kiss you.

3. A guy on the street says that you look great today.

4. Guys at school repeatedly make sexual comments to one of your friends.

5. A person writes sexual graffiti messages in the school bathroom about someone else.

Answers:

1. No. One sexist joke is not harassment. But a pattern of jokes or sexist language is.

2. Yes. If someone wants a sexual favor from you in exchange for something like a grade, it's sexual harassment. This happens most often when one person has more power than another does.

3. No. Not unless it makes you really uncomfortable or he says it in front of other guys in a way that isn't flirting, but designed to draw unwelcome attention to you.

4. Yes. There is a pattern here of unwanted behavior which your friend didn't ask for and doesn't enjoy.

5. Yes. Writing sexual messages about a person can ruin their reputation and creates a hostile environment that could make that person uncomfortable at school.

Hostile environment: This is complicated to define. It can include anything that creates an unpleasant or painful situation for another person, like (1) repeated sexual comments or advances or (2) repeated use of sexist language, or displaying sexually explicit material. Hostile environments can interfere with your right to get an education or to work.

Have You Been Harassed?

☆ "I've been harassed many times. One time I was walking home and a bunch of guys drinking beer were staring at me. Then one said, 'Hey baby, want to come home with me?' I felt disgusted and started walking faster. They started to laugh and another guy said, 'Forget about it man. She already came home with me!' I was pissed off and wish I could have kicked them in the balls!"

☆ "I wore a short skirt to school and all the guys were trying to touch my legs. At first it was funny and I was playing along. But then I started to get annoyed. I told them to stop it, but they kept going."

☆ "I'm big chested and each time I wear a tank top, all the guys want a hug. Or they find an excuse to try to touch me. Or even worse they try to look down my shirt and act like it's normal. I hate that shit cuz it's disrespectful."

☆ "Everybody calls me Bubblebutt. My butt is big and I can't help it. I'm constantly getting harassed at school, in the streets, even at work. It's like my butt is the only thing people see. All the guys automatically assume I'm a slut or a tramp. Even the girls!"

What to Do about Sexual Harassment

1. Ask the harasser to stop.

2. Tell the harasser how you feel by using powerful "I" statements like:

   > I feel uncomfortable when you do that.
   > I want you to stop saying those things.
   > I don't like it when you look at me or touch me like that.
   > I don't want you to do that again.

3. Stick up for a friend who's being sexually harassed and support her if she wants to say something to the harasser.

4. Tell someone in authority what's happening—a teacher, principal, or boss.

5. Write down everything he said and did and file a complaint at your school or job.

THINK

Sexual harassment was not always talked about or taken very seriously. But in 1991, a law professor named Anita Hill testified that her ex-boss—U.S. Supreme Court Justice Clarence Thomas—sexually harassed her by repeatedly asking her for a date and talking about pornography in front of her. Hill felt she couldn't do anything at the time; she was afraid if she complained it would hurt her job prospects. Yet a few years later Hill did speak out against Thomas when he was being considered for the Supreme Court. Hill's testimony paved the way for other women to speak out against sexual harassment today.

Interview with Jose, coordinator of Student Leaders Against Sexual Harassment (SLASH)

Q: How did SLASH begin?
A: It began as an after-school program. The object was for youth to select a problem that severely affected their families or community and start organizing for change. The students did a lot of research on things like drugs, gangs, lack of jobs, and violence against women. They selected violence against women to work on. Sexual harassment is something they saw every day at school.

Q: What exactly does SLASH do?
A: First the students researched the problem. We looked at school policies—what teachers and staff are trained to do about it. We interviewed principals and other administrators. Then we did a five-page survey of sample groups from three schools. We spent more than a year on research.

Once we put it together, the picture was frightening—no training for teachers and no standard procedures for dealing with sexual harassment. What we heard from students was that sexual harassment was happening everywhere in the school, including the classroom, and teachers really did nothing about it. Less than 5% of students reported the problem. By and large, most of the people being sexually harassed were young women.

Q: So what did you do?
A: We made contact with members of the school board. They were outraged by the findings and impressed by what the students did. They unanimously passed a resolution for sweeping change—to revamp and improve training for teachers. They appointed students to be part of a task force along with top administrators. The resolution calls for mandatory education. So now curriculums have to be created and the training needs to begin.

Q: What did the students discover about sexual harassment in the schools?
A: 58% of those who experienced sexual harassment said it happened in the classroom. And that's the most supervised setting, so that's really shocking. The most common form was verbal harassment. Also a significant number were sexually assaulted—grabbed, pushed against a locker, pulled into the bathroom.

Q: Is this only in high schools?
A:: Everywhere we go, it's really common to hear stories—a group of guys pull a girl into a bathroom, boys pull down other boys' gym shorts. The rate of sexual assault in schools is kind of frightening. There were two rapes at a middle school. There was a gang sexual assault. At one of the schools, the teacher said unwanted touching happens every day in some form or another. It's out of control.

Q: What does SLASH do to help stop sexual harassment?
A: The students were trained to be peer educators. The teachers were extremely happy to have resources to help. These students understand what sexual harassment is, and its consequences.

Q: What are positive ways to fight sexual harassment?
A: Don't be silent. There's a lot of fear around reporting sexual harassment—you could get in trouble with your friends, or you're scared your parents won't understand, or the teachers will blame you. It's important to speak up though so things will really change. More and more school districts are taking this seriously. It's a good time to speak up right now.

What is discrimination?

You play on a college sports team. The male athletes at your school each get their own locker. You have to share two lockers with two dozen other female teammates. The guys are given team T-shirts, travel bags, and jackets. You and the other young women on the team have to buy your own.

OR

You are a young woman of color who wants to go to a certain law school. You're denied because of your race. You take the case to the Supreme Court. You win: you're allowed to go to that law school. But you must sit in a special chair marked "colored" and you're kept separate from your classmates.

These stories are true. The first happened in the early 1970s. The second took place in the late 1950s. Both are examples of discrimination.

What You Can Do Legally

There are government agencies whose job it is to eliminate discrimination practices at school and in the workplace. You can fight discrimination in the courts, though filing a lawsuit is expensive and time-consuming. Speaking out—telling someone that you feel discriminated against and that they need to stop—often works. If not, you can find out more about your options from the Equal Employment Opportunity Commission (EEOC) and the Office of Civil Rights of the Department of Education (OCR).

Six Ways to Fight Discrimination

1. Object to racist, sexist, ethnic, and other discriminatory jokes or comments. Speak up—your silence can be read as approval.

2. Organize different forums for getting to know other cultures. Make a commitment to learn about people from other races and cultures, and share yours with others.

3. Write Letters to the Editor when you see racial and gender stereotypes in the media. Don't watch movies or TV shows that you find offensive. Seek out alternative media sources.

4. Speak out when people say or do things that are biased—even if you aren't the target. They may not be aware that what they're saying is discriminatory.

5. Join human rights or community-based organizations in your area.

6. Support institutions and companies that promote racial inclusion. Boycott stores or businesses that don't.

How Do You Define Discrimination?

☆ "Discrimination is when someone sets limits on you because of the way you look, speak, or act, or because of your height, weight, or skin color. It's very unfair."

☆ "Discrimination is when someone treats you bad or doesn't give you opportunities to show who you really are. They don't like you so you can't get a job or into school. It's almost like prejudice except that when someone discriminates against you it's usually because they have some sort of power over you."

☆ "When someone doesn't let you in a school club because of your sex, color, race, or body type or 'cause you can't speak the language they do."

☆ "I think discrimination is when someone leaves you out because of your skin color, the way you look, or what class you're in (upper, middle, lower)."

☆ "Discrimination is when someone hates another for just being herself, living her life with whoever she wants."

☆ "Discrimination is when you're being judged in a negative way. Because of this judgment, it could affect how you interact with people, how easily you can find a job, etc."

What Is Discrimination?

discrimination: Denial of equality based on personal characteristics like race, sex, sexual orientation, religion, or age.

-ism: Discrimination on the basis of _____. You can fill in the blank: sex, race, age, class, religion, sexual orientation.

stereotype: A mental or verbal bias, usually negative, about a group of people based on identifying factors like class, race, religion, sexual orientation, or other group affiliation.

prejudice: Literally means to "pre-judge" someone based on certain ideas or stereotypes.

Proposition 21

In 2000, California voters approved Proposition 21, also known as the Gang Violence and Juvenile Crime Prevention Act, which:

✳ Makes it easier to try, sentence, and imprison youths as adults

✳ Unseals confidential juvenile records

✳ Expands the definition of a "gang" to mean an informal group of three or more people

✳ Funnels money away from rehabilitation of youth, and towards incarceration.

In 1971, before Title IX . . .

✳ 2% of women participated in college athletics.

✳ 294,000 young women played high school sports.

✳ The average college budgeted less than a dollar a year for each female athlete.

✳ Women received 9% of all medical degrees.

✳ Women received 7% of all law degrees.

After Title IX

✳ In 1997, 36% of women participated in college athletics.

✳ In 1992, 2 million young women played high school sports.

✳ Colleges and universities now spend $4,100 a year for each female athlete.

✳ In 1994, women received 38% of all medical degrees.

✳ In 1994, women received 43% of all law degrees.

Have You Ever Been Discriminated Against?

☆ "So many times I can't remember!"

☆ "A girl in middle school who was nice to me (and Hispanic) asked me if I was Hispanic. When I told her no, she began asking me if I was French, Italian, Greek, etc. When I told her I was Palestinian, she gave me a dirty look and has been mean to me ever since."

☆ "When I went to the hospital to find out if I was pregnant, the woman asked me how old I was and shook her head as if she was thinking—young black females having babies at an early age."

☆ "I was discriminated against at a supermarket cuz I am Hispanic. The cashier let a white lady cut me in line, and I was next! I complained about it. But nobody cared. I'm never going back."

☆ "It was September 16, Mexican Independence Day. I had my flag on a table and a girl walked by and hit my flag so I mugged her. Her friend told her, 'Hey, she mugged you.' She came back getting an attitude with me and said, 'Why you look at me that way?' like she was going to do something. I said, 'Cause you disrespected me and my country.' She said, 'So.' I said, 'Well, did I do anything to you? So why did you do that?' She stayed quiet and walked away."

Legal Highlights on the Road to Equality

1920: Women get the right to vote with the passage of the 19th Amendment. This is also the first year of the Miss America Pageant!

1963: Equal Pay Act (EPA) is passed, forbidding companies from paying women less than men for doing the same work.

1964: Civil Rights Act is passed, prohibiting discrimination at work and federally funded schools on the basis of race, gender, national origin, religion, or pregnancy.

1972: Title IX, part of the Education Amendments, prohibits gender discrimination in schools that receive federal money, which are most schools, both public and private.

Interview with Shirley, 18, a youth activist

Numerous youth and community-based groups worked together in California for two years to inform people about Proposition 21 before it came on the ballot. It passed in 2000. Youth advocacy groups, working with the ACLU and the League of Women Voters, continue to band together to fight the implementation of the Proposition.

Q: Why did you get involved with activist work?
A: Prop 21 is just ridiculous. It targets people of color and doesn't give youth a chance to rehabilitate. If you did something at 14 and you think your file will be erased at 18, it's not true anymore. It'll count as a strike against you.

The people who wrote Prop 21, it wouldn't affect them or their kids. It wasn't preventing a problem, it was making it worse because all they're doing is creating hardened criminals out of young boys and girls.

Q: What did you do when you got involved in protesting?
A: I went to workshops to learn about Prop 21 and I did trainings to learn how to tell about it.

Q: What did you learn from doing this work?
A: That when something as ridiculous as Prop 21 affects a whole community, people can unite and fight against it without having to worry about gangs or fights or enemies or color.

With the money it takes to send someone to prison for one year, you can send people to college for four. There'd be no need to build ten more prisons for all the people they won't have to arrest.

Q: How did people work together?
A: There were a lot of rallies and one big rally at a school that lasted a whole day. At the rallies, there were workshops. A lot of people were educated about it.

Q: How did it make you feel to get involved with fighting Prop 21?
A: As a youth, I have to stand up for myself. Like when you go to the army, you fight for your country. I'm fighting for my youth and for my kids' future and people I care about and people who I don't know whose lives are being thrown away when they aren't given a second chance.

What are my rights as an immigrant?

What's It Like to Come from Another Country?

by Diana, 16

There are so many things I learned about immigration. Like if you leave the U.S., it will be hard to come back in. At first, when we got here, my brother and I complained, "We don't like it here. It sucks. We want to go back home. It's so cold here. Back home, it's warm." We had to start over: We had no toys, no bed. We had to sleep on the floor.

Then school started. We hated it. There was no way to communicate with the teachers—they all spoke English. No kids would play with me because I couldn't speak English. My mom cried. One time my brother, sister, and I were so hungry that my mom took us to McDonald's. Not knowing any English, it took us awhile to order something. But people were patient with us.

Ten years later, my dad became a citizen. And that meant that we could get our passports stamped as residents. One week later, we went back to Mexico. I was so happy to see my grandma who I hadn't seen in a long time.

Immigration Definitions

Immigration and Naturalization Service: The INS is a branch of government that enforces immigration laws and distributes forms for naturalization.

Naturalization: The process by which immigrants can become citizens.

Permanent resident: Having the legal right to live and work in the U.S. You have to be a permanent resident for a certain number of years to become a citizen, and permanent residents who want to become citizens are restricted from leaving the U.S. for long periods of time.

Permanent resident card: Also known as a "Green Card," this document is evidence of permanent residence status.

Undocumented immigrant: A non-citizen with no card to show permanent residence status.

RESOURCES

Bureau of Citizenship and Immigration Services (formerly the Immigration and Naturalization Service (INS))
www.immigration.gov/
1-800-375-5283

National Network for Immigrant and Refugee Rights
www.nnirr.org/
510-465-1984

Dear Homegirl,

My best friend came here from Vietnam a few months ago. No one in her family is a citizen. I was born here. My friend wants to know if she has the right to go to school like I do. Does she?

Dear Helpful,

Yes. Anyone living in the United States is entitled to a lot of the same rights as other citizens, including a right to an education. It doesn't matter if they're undocumented or without papers. Like you, your friend has the right to a free public education and access to all the programs your school has to offer.

Being an Immigrant Is Never Easy

by Faye, 16

As an immigrant in the USA, I feel happy because I can know another big country in the world. I feel sad because I can't speak good English. I feel more comfortable speaking Chinese because it is my first language, and I have been speaking it for almost 17 years.

I had a very hard time when I first came here. Many things here are different from China. My parents needed to find jobs to get money, my brothers and I had to go to an American school. We needed to know how to take the bus, and where we could get food. No one helped us. We had to stand up for ourselves. As an immigrant, it's hard to find a good job, hard to go to a good school, hard to do everything well.

My parents don't speak English well, so it's very difficult for them to adapt here. I have to translate for them. When my mom went to the hospital, or when my parents went to a meeting at my brothers' school, I translated for them. I was very nervous, and I made a lot of mistakes. I felt very hot in my face. It made me make up my mind to study hard in school to learn more English.

The reason we came here was because my parents wanted us to go to good colleges, then get good jobs. As an immigrant young woman, I face more hard situations here than I would in China. Sometimes I just want to die or go back to China. Sometimes I just give up because I feel it's too difficult to learn English. It's hard for me to adapt, but I will try! That's what life looks like, right?

Is It Worth It?

Advantages of becoming a U.S. citizen:

○ You can vote if you are over 18.

○ You can apply for jobs with the federal government.

○ You can bring your immediate family members to the U.S. without a long wait.

○ You can travel outside of the U.S. without losing your citizenship.

Disadvantages of becoming a U.S. citizen:

○ You must take an oath of allegiance and that means saying you are no longer loyal to your native country.

○ You may lose your right to vote in your native country.

○ You may need a work permit to work in your native country.

○ You may lose citizenship in your native country.

○ You must pass basic English language and U.S. government and history tests that you have to study for.

Becoming a Citizen

Q: If my parents get their citizenship, do I automatically get mine?
A: Yes. If you're under 18 and one or both of your parents are naturalized, permanent residents, you can get your citizenship through them. You need to be:

☆ under 18 AND unmarried OR

☆ a permanent resident and under legal custody of a parent who is a citizen OR

☆ not a permanent resident, but you have a citizen parent who has lived in the U.S. for at least five years, two of those years after your 14th birthday.

You would fill out a form (N-600) "Application for a Certificate of Citizenship," which you can get from the INS. And you'll have to take an Oath of Allegiance to the U.S. (This can be waived if you are very young.) If you are 18 or over, you fill out a different form (N-400) "Application for Naturalization."

Q: How long does it take to get naturalized?
A: It varies. The process can take many years; the average is about ten, though the INS claims they are working to speed things up.

Q: What are the steps involved in naturalization?
A: The process of becoming a U.S. citizen can be long and difficult. You have to be a permanent resident for at least five years first, you have to be of "good moral character," and not have committed any crimes. Then, in addition to filling out the right forms, you are:

☆ photographed

☆ fingerprinted

☆ interviewed to prove that you understand, speak, and write English by answering questions about U.S. history

☆ sworn to defend and support the U.S. Constitution by taking an "Oath of Allegiance."

Q: Where can I go for help with immigration and naturalization?
A: Immigrating to another country, finding work, and becoming naturalized can be challenging and intimidating. See the Resources on page 76.

How do i prepare for college?

Good grades and good scores on standardized tests will help you get into college. But these numbers are just some of the things that colleges look at. Your interests, volunteer work, and activities outside of school also add up to make you stand out from other applicants.

Most schools ask you to write a personal essay. Let your personality come through by writing about your background, your family, the culture or groups you belong to—anything that shows who you really are besides test scores. Many college applicants sound the same, but college admissions officers also want to read about interesting people.

What are the SATs and ACTs and how do i prepare for them?

SAT stands for Scholastic Aptitude Test. ACT Assessment stands for American College Testing Assessment. These tests are created by

the Educational Testing Service (ETS), a large, nonprofit company in New Jersey.

SAT I: This three-hour test measures verbal and math reasoning. It's supposed to predict how you will do in your first year of college. Many four-year colleges require the test for admission. Scored on a scale from 400 to 1600.

SAT II: This one-hour test in a subject area like foreign language, history, or biology is not required by all colleges. Check with the admissions office.

Choosing a College

Private universities, single-sex schools, religious colleges, military colleges... There are hundreds of schools for you to choose from. While it may feel that where you go to college depends more on a school accepting you, in reality you can take a lot of control for the decision. Think about interviewing the schools you want to apply to by asking yourself questions to see which schools fit your needs.

1. Does the school offer the programs and courses I'm interested in?

2. Does the school have an acceptable ratio of female to male professors? What percentage of these professors are people of color?

3. Does the college offer major or minor programs in women's studies or ethnic studies, or other courses related to the history and importance of minority groups?

4. What kind of health care is available for students?

5. Is there child care on campus?

6. Are there groups or organizations that fit my interests?

7. What kinds of sports teams and facilities are there?

8. Is the price of this education reasonable for what I would get?

9. Do I want to commute to a local college or live away from home?

10. Do I want to go to college in a city or a small college town?

11. Is there a significant number of students like me (ethnic, gay, or religious) so that I won't feel isolated?

If possible, arrange an on-campus interview to talk to someone in the admissions office. Or just go by yourself and walk around to get a feel for the school. Most current students are happy to talk to you about their experiences if you ask.

TIPS

Taking Standardized Tests

* Read all directions carefully so you understand what you're supposed to do.

* Do the easier questions first.

* Don't spend too much time on any single question. Skip a hard question and come back later.

* Eliminate wrong answers. If you can cross out two of four possible answers, you have a 50-50 chance of picking the right one.

* Stay cool. It's just a test.

Standardized Test Biases

While many colleges use tests like the SAT and ACT to screen college applicants, you should know that these tests, particularly the SAT, are not fair measures of your abilities. The SAT is gender-, race-, and class-biased. Studies by the College Board show that young women score an average of 40 points lower than their male counterparts on this test—even though they get higher grades in high school and college. Youth of color and immigrants also score consistently lower than white students, as do lower income students.

What You Can Do About It

Look for SAT-optional colleges that don't require standardized test scores. Or take the ACT, which is based on your high school courses. The gender bias is not as great as it is on the SAT.

If you're applying to a school that requires the SAT, do as much preparation as you can to raise your test scores. Prep courses are very expensive, but there are free online services that you can use. Either way, the trick is to do as many practice tests as you can before the real thing.

FACTS

* California has the largest system of community colleges in the world.
* Currently, 2.9 million students attend community colleges in the state.

PSAT: A test you usually take during junior year of high school. It's a practice SAT that measures critical reading, math, and writing skills. If you do really well, you may be eligible for a National Merit Scholarship, which can help pay for college.

ACT: A standardized test required by some colleges for admissions. Unlike the SAT, the questions are based directly on high school subjects: English, math, reading, and science reasoning. Scored on a scale from 4 to 36.

TOEFL: A test to measure your English language abilities. It's a good idea to take this test if your first language isn't English and you're planning to go to a U.S. college or university.

Fee Waivers: It costs money to take these tests, but don't let the price keep you from taking them. Many schools offer waivers to some students so you don't have to pay the fees. See your school counselor to apply.

Different Types of Colleges

Community Colleges

What they are: CCs are publicly supported colleges that lead to a two-year Associate's Degree.

Requirements: By law, these colleges must admit any resident over 18 with or without a high school diploma, any non-resident who has a high school diploma or the equivalent, and current high school students (with approval) who want to take advanced placement courses.

What they offer: Remedial instruction, English as a second language, certificate programs in fields such as health and technology, job training skills, and adult education.

Benefits: Offer transfer programs to four-year schools. Many students attend CCs for two years to fulfill requirements or brush up on skills, then transfer to more expensive universities to get their baccalaureate degrees. Check with counseling services at your community college and with the admissions office at the school to which you want to transfer in order to be sure that the courses you take at CC will be accepted. CCs also offer flexible scheduling—day, night, and weekend courses.

Expenses: Fees are usually very low for residents. For example, at City College of San Francisco the cost is $11 per credit. Non-residents are charged slightly higher fees.

Important: You can get a fee waiver, that is the Board of Governors will pay your enrollment fees, if you are a low-income state resident. Check with the financial aid office or guidance counselor at your school.

State Schools

What they are: Four-year colleges connected through a state university system. Each campus has unique characteristics and sometimes slightly different admissions requirements.

Requirements: High school diploma or GED and satisfactory completion of college prep courses in high school. For the California State University system, for example, you'll need:
- ✔ English (four years)
- ✔ Math (three years)
- ✔ U.S. History (one year)
- ✔ Lab Science (one year)
- ✔ Foreign Language (two years)
- ✔ Other electives

What they offer: Undergraduate degrees like B.A. (Bachelor of Arts) and graduate degrees like M.A. (Master of Arts) or M.S. (Master of Science).

Benefits: State university systems usually offer a wide choice of majors and fields of study.

Expenses: Fees are higher than at community colleges but lower than at private universities. Out-of-state residents pay fees and tuition. Residents pay fees but not tuition.

Universities

What they are: Four-year universities consisting of a number of different smaller colleges. Universities can be public (they get money from the state government) or private.

Requirements: Like state colleges, it's mandatory to take several years in each subject, but it's strongly recommended that you take an additional year of each to be competitive.

What they offer: Undergraduate degrees like B.A. (Bachelor of Arts), B.S. (Bachelor of Science), other four-year degrees in specialty areas, and graduate degrees like M.A. (Master of Arts), M.S. (Master of Science) and Ph.D. (Doctor of Philosophy).

Benefits: Universities usually have better academic reputations than state colleges. They attract top professors in their fields. A degree from a top university is often prestigious and it might mean more to some future employers or graduate programs.

Expenses: Private tuition is much higher than state schools. At public universities, out-of-state students pay higher fees than in-state students do.

How do i pay for college?

Financial aid is money given to a student and/or the family to help pay for education. Financial aid comes in two forms: gift aid, like grants and scholarships, which doesn't need to be repaid, or self-help aid like loans and work-study programs.

Your family is expected to contribute to your education. This is called your Expected Family Contribution (EFC). The exact amount is determined by a federal formula that takes into consideration your family's income; assets like savings and checking accounts; benefits like unemployment, Social Security, or alimony payments; family size; number of family members in college; and your dependency status. The EFC is used in figuring out your eligibility for federal, need-based aid by subtracting the EFC amount from the cost of attendance to come up with your financial need.

If you don't expect your family to contribute to your education, things get a bit tricky. Declaring yourself to be legally emancipated is not enough to release your parents or guardians from being responsible for providing for your education. If it were that easy, every parent would "divorce" their children before sending them to college. The financial aid rules for independent status are much stricter, although situations like family members' being out of work, high medical expenses, or the death of a parent clearly would affect your ability to pay for your education. Talk to your school's financial aid advisor about any of these kinds of circumstances to see how they might be able to help.

What's EOP?

Most colleges have an Educational Opportunity Program (EOP) that supports low-income youth from the time they enter college until they graduate.

EOP offers:
- ✔ help getting financial aid
- ✔ tutoring services for classes
- ✔ study groups
- ✔ workshops to help pass tests
- ✔ personal, career, and academic advising
- ✔ advocacy for any problems you might have at college with professors, classes, etc.

You apply for EOP support at the same time you apply for college. On most applications, there's a box that asks if you want to be considered for EOP. Check "yes" and they'll send you a separate application.

The application asks about your educational experiences and you and your family's

Grants and Scholarships

Supplemental Educational Opportunity Grants (SEOG): Government grant for low-income students, particularly those whose families cannot contribute.

Scholarships: Money from different organizations and sponsors based on things like your academic, athletic, leadership, or artistic talents, financial need, whether you belong to an under-represented gender or ethnic group, or have some other special interest in a subject or field of study.

You may have to do some investigating to find out about applying for scholarships. Here are some places to check:

- ☆ **high school guidance counselor**
- ☆ **local library**
- ☆ **college financial aid office**

Internet sites like www.fastweb.com match your background to a scholarship database and tell you what you may be eligible for.

Warning: Don't pay money to find out about scholarships. If an agency or person wants your money to search for money, it's usually a scam.

Make the Process Easier

✳ Make yourself seen in the financial aid office at the college where you're thinking of applying. Find out the location, their hours, and identify a friendly person to talk to. Don't hesitate to go to them for help.

✳ Talk to a guidance counselor at your high school, especially if you're applying to a college that's far away.

✳ Try not to get discouraged. The first time you fill out all the forms is always the hardest. And if you make a mistake, you don't lose out—they just send it back to you to be corrected. Be sure to watch your mail and respond quickly.

✳ Talk to your brother or sister, or your friends' older brothers or sisters—anyone who has already been through the application process. They can help you get through the paperwork.

income. You will also be asked to provide two letters of recommendation. Letters from teachers, church members, advisors, adult friends, or coaches are all fine. Ask someone who knows you well and who can write about how you stand out from the crowd and why it's important that you get a college education.

EOP support is mostly based on income. If your family income is too high, you won't be eligible. If you don't qualify for EOP, most colleges have something like Student Outreach Services or Dean's Offices where you can go for advice on everything from finding the library to deciding what classes to take.

How much money do i need for college?

You'll need enough money to cover the following expenses:
- ✔ tuition and fees
- ✔ rent and utilities
- ✔ food, clothing, and personal items
- ✔ transportation
- ✔ books, notepads, pens, and other supplies
- ✔ miscellaneous expenses

Getting money for college can take a lot of research and filling out of forms. The process can be a little frustrating and intimidating, but there are hotline numbers to call and financial aid offices at all colleges to help you figure things out. When you do get money for school, it makes all the paperwork worth it.

Applying for Financial Aid

All state schools and many colleges require you to fill out a form called FAFSA—Free Application for Federal Student Aid. It helps them determine how much money to give you and from what sources. You can get the form from places like:
- ✔ high school guidance counselor
- ✔ college financial aid office
- ✔ on the Internet at www.fafsa.ed.gov
- ✔ call 1-800-4-FED-AID

Check with the college where you're applying to see if they require any other financial aid forms.

To fill out the FAFSA, you'll need your social security number and a copy of your parents' tax return form and a copy of yours if you file on your own. You must show a copy of your parents' tax return—even if you think they aren't going to help you with school.

You apply for financial aid after January 1st and before July for the following school year. Check with colleges to find out the specific deadlines. Filling out these forms can be stressful and time consuming. Call the federal hotline number at 1-800-4-FED-AID for help. Or visit a financial aid officer at the college where you're applying, or talk to your high school guidance counselor. It's hard to do this on your own, especially the first time.

Every year that you're in school, you'll fill out a new form. You may get more money if you have brothers or sisters in school or if your financial circumstances change.

Student Loans and Work-Study

Stafford Loans: You borrow money under your own name. There is no credit check for this loan. The federal government will pay the interest while you're going to school, and you pay it back after you graduate or start going to school less than half-time.

Federal Perkins Loans: Based on exceptional financial need. You can get up to $4,000 a year for school. You apply through the financial aid office of your school. The money comes from the federal government and your college gives you the check. The interest rate is lower than Stafford Loans and there are better repayment options.

Federal Pell Grants: This is a loan given by the government based on financial need. You can get up to $3,125 each year depending on things like the cost of your college, whether you are going full- or part-time, and how much, if anything, your family can contribute. This is one of the best grants you can get and it's especially good for low-income youth because there is a very low interest rate when you start paying it back.

Plus Loans: Allow your parents to borrow money for you to help finance college costs.

(All loans have a grace period—the time when you don't have to begin paying back your loans, usually six months after school ends. The grace period lets you find a job and get on your feet financially without worrying about monthly loan payments.)

Federal Work-Study: A part-time job, usually working at the school, that's part of your financial aid package. Your pay is subsidized by the federal government, so employers have a financial incentive to hire you over other students.

How do i find a job i'll like?

A first step in thinking about a job is to know yourself—your interests, skills, and values. A fun way to find out about yourself is to take a career interests quiz. You can find the quizzes online or in your school library or any career guidebook. By answering a series of questions like the ones at the top of the next page, you are then matched with possible career choices. Try taking several tests, because they're each a little different. Then you'll get a more complete picture of possible careers to match your interests.

Another way to do self-assessment is to observe yourself and see what you're comfortable doing. Talking to people you know who are happy with their jobs can also give you lots of information.

There's a difference between having a job and developing a career. Jobs are where you work to get paid to do your best. Careers are paths to growth where you combine skills, knowledge, and experience to create a fulfilling lifestyle for yourself. A series of jobs can lead to a career, so if you don't know exactly what career you want right now, it's okay. You can work at different jobs, add to your experience, and decide later.

How do i get a job?

Looking for a job is a job in itself.

Finding a job takes organizational skills, focus, and the ability to sell yourself. Looking for work can also be emotionally hard. It's difficult to make phone calls or talk to people you don't know. It's also easy to get discouraged if you don't get a job you want. You might even start to doubt yourself or your abilities.

Places to look for jobs:

✔ friends and word-of-mouth

✔ newspapers and magazines

✔ career centers and job fairs at high schools, colleges, etc.

✔ the Internet

How to fight the looking-for-a-job blues:

✔ Talk to other young people who are looking for work. Share stories so you see you're not alone.

✔ Talk to family and friends who can remind you that you're worthy and competent.

✔ Reward yourself for trying. Buy some small treat, get some exercise, do something nice for yourself. You deserve it.

What's a resume?

You'll need a resume for most jobs. A resume is a summary of your skills and background presented in a brief format. It gives future employers a quick way to see your skills and qualifications. Think of it as an advertisement for yourself.

When you think about doing a resume, you might get nervous. Try not to think of it as a chore, but a chance to show yourself. There are several ways to write a resume, but the ideal one is easy-to-read and tailored to the job you're applying for. You may have to do a few versions with some slight changes, but it's worth it.

✔ There is no one right resume. But some things can work against you.

✔ Don't include your birthdate, height, weight, marital status, or social security number.

✔ Don't include your references, but make sure to have them ready if asked.

✔ Be sure to include dates.

✔ Watch for misspellings and typos.

✔ Avoid fuzzy or vague language.

✔ Don't use colored paper (other than beige) or a lot of fancy fonts. Keep it simple.

✔ If you're searching for jobs online and are emailing your resume, it's a good idea to email it to yourself first to see what it looks like and make sure the formatting stays the same.

Sample Resume

Your name
Address
City, State, Zip Code
Phone number
email

Objective: Clear statement of position you're seeking. Have only one for each resume, like "To gain a position as..."

Skills:

Reliable and hard working

Excellent written and verbal communication skills

Works well individually or in a group

Has general office skills including telephones, copying, faxing, typing, and basic computer skills

Speaks Spanish fluently

Work and Volunteer Experience:

Office Assistant, Dr. Smith's Dental Office, June-August 1999.

Member, Young Women's Work Project, September 1999-present.

Caretaker for children, 1994–present.

Education: Currently attending [name of your school here].

References available upon request.

(Adapted from Young Woman's Work Project)

The Cover Letter

A cover letter can help get your resume read out of the hundreds of others that may be sitting on an employer's desk. The cover letter specifies what position you're applying for, what your accomplishments are, why an employer should call you for an interview, and what you could add to the company or organization if you were hired.

Staying Organized

Keep a notebook to list when and where you've sent your resumes and the job that you applied for. After a couple of weeks, make follow-up phone calls and write down what's said—most importantly, when you should get back in touch. It may feel strange to call people you don't know. But it gets easier as time goes by, and you can always practice before you make the call.

TIPS

Cover Letters

✳ Tailor the letter so it shows you've done some research and are familiar with the organization.

✳ Address it to a specific person, rather than just "Human Resources" or "Personnel."

✳ Keep paragraphs short.

✳ Write about specific things you've done or problems you've solved that are related to the position.

✳ Don't be modest—this is your chance to shine!

✳ Ask for an interview and make sure to include your name and phone number.

✳ Sometimes it's hard to be objective about yourself, so show your letters to a few people for feedback. A good reader can tell you if you're being too modest and shy or if you haven't conveyed a clear sense of who you are and what you've accomplished.

Resumes

Use assertive language when writing your resume. The following words show powerful actions:

achieved	administrated
controlled	coordinated
counseled	developed
examined	initiated
in charge of	managed
organized	planned
researched	responsible for
set up	trained
wrote	

Skills can be:

✳ something you've learned like computers

✳ something you're good at like writing or math

✳ personality traits like creative or hard working

✳ something you got because of your life experiences—such as knowing a language or leadership ability

Interview with Susie at the San Francisco Museum of Modern Art (SFMOMA)

Q: Can you describe your job?
A: I design and produce educational websites and computer stations in the museum that teach about art.

Q: What do you like about your job?
A: I like teaching people about the new interactive medium. I get to work with writers and scholars. They know a lot about art history, but they don't necessarily know very much about interactive media. I work with them so our team can use their information in new and exciting ways.

Q: How did you get into your job?
A: Four years ago I started working as a production assistant for an interactive media company. I learned about making educational CD-ROMs for children. I got very excited about designing computer games for kids. I took some extra classes at San Francisco State University's multimedia studies program. I kept working and was learning constantly about computers and technology as well as how to design effective education projects. I was lucky to have two very good mentors who let me take on more and more responsibility.

I heard about the job at SFMOMA and thought, "Wow!" This job allows me to combine a number of my interests with a lot of responsibility and gives me tons of room to grow and learn new things.

Q: Does your job help the community?
A: It helps young people in general because it shows ways that art can open new worlds in people's lives.

Q: Did you ever think about changing careers?
A: I feel like my career is about constant change. I often see forks in the road and have to decide which career direction to go in. It's exciting because I also know that if I take one path, others will still be there if I want to put the energy into exploring them. I know I want to stay in a career that feels creative and has a teaching component to it.

Q: What advice would you give to young women looking for a job?
A: Don't be afraid of taking a path where you don't know the outcome. Always remember that you are smart and creative and deserve respect.

How do i manage my money?

Money doesn't equal happiness or power. It's your relationship to money—how you feel about it and use it in the world—that gives you power over your money. Take the quiz to the right to see how you relate to money.

How can i budget my money?

Being aware of how you spend money each week will give you a lot of information about your financial habits. First, write down everything you spend—every dollar on soda, gum, bus fare, and gifts. Here's how to do it:

Keep a spending log for a week. Write what you actually spend—not what you think you should be spending.

Figure out your monthly expenses. Look through your weekly spending log to help you figure this out. Multiply your weekly expenses for certain things (like food) by four and organize them into general categories. You can use the categories below or make up ones that fit your lifestyle. Try to list everything you can and include money each month for things like gifts or vacation. It'll be easier to find out what you realistically spend and need this way.

> **Food:**
> **Clothing:**
> **Transportation:**
> **Rent or housing:**
> **Entertainment (like cable, movies, clubs):**
> **Phone bill/pager bill:**
> **Debt or credit card payment:**
> **Laundry:**
> **Charitable giving:**
> **Gifts:**
> **Travel:**
> **Books, newspapers, magazines:**
> **TOTAL:**

Write down your monthly income, then subtract your monthly expenses. See if you spend more money than you earn or if you have money left over after your expenses. Either way, making and spending money is within your control. Financial stability is not something that comes from outside, but rather starts with being aware of your own relationship to money.

How can i open a bank account?

By law you have to be over 18 to enter into a contract, and a checking account counts as a contract between you and a bank. So, if you are under 18, you'll need a parent or guardian's signature to open a checking account. This means that they are legally responsible for your use of the account and any checks you write. If you are under 18, you can open a savings account without your parents, but you have to have identification and your Social Security card.

Many banks today will also offer you a credit card (MasterCard or Visa) with your checking account. Be careful to read the fine print on the agreement that comes with these cards. Interest rates are usually very high—near 20%. If you miss just one payment, the rate can go up even higher.

Credit cards are designed to get you to spend money. Think about spending cash instead of charging when you go to buy something—see if you have enough. If you don't, are you willing to pay an extra 20% to charge it? That would be an extra $4 on a $20 item. Try not to get sucked into debt. It's easy to get into,

Eight Ways to Save Money

1. Make your own fun container for all your loose change.
2. Only take as much cash as you need so you aren't tempted to spend more.
3. Shop around for bargains.
4. Take your lunch to school instead of buying it.
5. Sell or trade clothes you never wear or don't like anymore.
6. Put money away somewhere where you can't get to it easily.
7. Make your own school yearbook by taking pictures of your friends.
8. Put a certain amount, like 10% of your wages, into a savings account on a regular basis.

Faye's Budget for One Week

Here's an example of Faye's income and expenses for one week. Knowing how she spends money can help her plan for the month:

Income for one week	
Part-time job:	$140
Other:	$30
Total Income:	**$170**

Expenses for one week	
Eating out:	$30
Snacks and drinks:	$10
Personal stuff:	$30
Clothing:	$85
Other:	$10
Total Expenses:	**$165**

Balance My Budget	
Total income:	$170
Total expenses:	$165
Difference:	**$5**

> "My credit card limit is $600. I went over the limit. It was not good because I couldn't use the card again until I returned the money. But as long as I put the money back, I can use it again! And after using it for six months, I got a higher credit limit, something like $1,200. The advice I want to give people is don't spend over the limited amount. You will get bad credit and you will be charged a lot!"
>
> Faye, 16

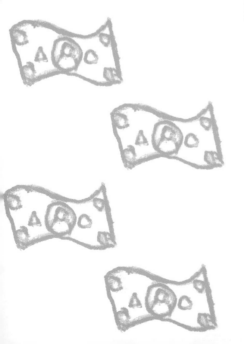

What's Your Money Personality

(Adapted from the Women's Financial Network)

1. If someone left me $10,000 my first reaction would be:
   a. To go out and spend it on things for myself and gifts for others.
   b. To feel overwhelmed and not make any decisions about it.
   c. To not touch the money right away, but open up a bank account and let it accumulate interest.

2. Here's how I deal with a budget:
   a. I don't budget. I buy what I want whenever I want it.
   b. I keep meaning to budget my money one day, but it seems too much for me.
   c. I keep reworking my budget and hardly spend any money at all.

3. My attitude towards credit cards is:
   a. I use them to buy what I want and I try to pay the minimum balance.
   b. I use them but I don't think about my balance very often. I sometimes forget to make payments.
   c. I never use credit cards, or use them as little as possible.

4. When it comes to keeping a record of my bills:
   a. I keep records sometimes, but often I can't find them.
   b. I don't even know what records to keep, so I don't keep any.
   c. I keep very careful records and I know where every dollar is.

5. My financial goals are:
   a. To have enough money so I can always buy what I want.
   b. I don't think about goals too much, so I don't think I have any.
   c. To make a lot of money and make sure I always have it.

If you answered mostly "a" to these questions, you may be a Spender. If you answered mostly "b" then you could be an Avoider. And if you answered mostly "c" you may have some Super Saver traits.

The Spender: You love to spend money on whatever you like. You have a hard time holding onto money or budgeting it. You think about money only in the short term, not for long-term goals.

The Avoider: You would prefer to think about anything else but money. You avoid managing or budgeting money. You feel anxious or incompetent about money.

The Super Saver: You like to hold onto money. You don't want to spend it on yourself or anyone else. Maybe you fear money, so you hold onto it.

You probably have characteristics of all of these types. Different money personalities may surface at different times. That's normal. Recognizing your relationship to money—what fears or anxieties you have about it—is the first step towards taking control. Practicing some of the following things can also help:

If you are an **Avoider**, you can. . .
Sit down and write out specific financial goals for the future.
Keep track of everything you spend for a week.

If you are a **Spender**, you can. . .
Open a savings account and put some money away.
Do something fun (besides shopping) where you don't have to spend money.

If you are a **Super Saver**, you can. . .
Buy a small gift for you or a friend.
Write down all the times you think about money for a week and see when you're anxious or fearful about it.

How do i plan my future?

Some say it's fate or destiny. Others say it's all what you make of it. It's probably a little bit of both. For the part of your future that you can control, it may take some time and effort to figure out what you want.

Powerful Women

Power is powerful. Sometimes it's negative when people use it to dominate and restrict others. Power can mean knowing yourself and what you want, expressing your creativity, getting involved with people and causes you believe in, or demonstrating leadership and other special skills.

Using power, showing off skills, going for what you want, and competing may make you uncomfortable or lead to conflict. It can get you labeled as someone who thinks too much of herself or someone who wants too much. So rather than risk criticism, you may bury your desire for power.

But power is not about popularity, though it may seem that way sometimes. Power is about knowing yourself and using that knowledge in the world. Power doesn't require anyone else's approval. It's not a dirty word, it's one that you have the right to claim and use.

Listen to Your Words

Several years ago, Robin Lakoff, a linguistics professor, noticed several things about the way women speak that differed from the way men do. She found that instead of saying something like, "It's hot today," women were more likely to say, "It's hot today, isn't it?" They added a tag like "isn't it" that turned their statements into questions.

Lakoff also found that women's voices sounded less sure than men's did. They often said things like, "It will be ready around 7," that sounded more like, "It will be ready around 7, if that's okay with you."

This could mean that women want approval when they speak. Or that they aren't sure of how their demands or statements will be received so they ask them as questions.

What about your own word patterns? Do you say something in the form of a question when you mean to state it as a matter of fact? Do you and your friends speak differently from guys? What's the difference? Saying what you know with authority is one way to express your power.

THINK

Your Future

* Who are the people you respect? Why?

* What kind of friends do you want around? What are their qualities?

* What do you need money for? How do you like to spend your money?

* What kinds of work would be meaningful to you?

* What are your goals now? What are your goals five years from now?

* Where can you find help to meet these goals?

"The thing that I like about working with other young women is that all of us are different, have different backgrounds, different neighborhoods, and have so many different ideas to make one good idea."

Sheryl, 17

"By us making this book it allows young women to be educated from our experiences and to be proud of being a woman. Seeing what a generation has done before their time may encourage them to do something even more triumphant and powerful."

Aisha, 19

Describe the woman you are becoming.

☆ "I guess I'm still growing and will continue to grow. I'm learning and becoming wiser and more aware of people's feelings and emotions. I'm learning to smile more. I'm becoming more confident and independent."

☆ "The woman I am becoming is strong, independent, reliable, and successful."

☆ "I think I'm just growing up and learning how to solve problems in my life. Maybe I'll become more mature, maybe I'll be the same—still like a kid."

☆ "I am becoming enthusiastic about the future because of all the things I'm learning every day. I think my experiences are making me stronger and smarter. I want to use this strength and knowledge to help others."

☆ "I'm educating myself and learning about who I am and what I wanna be. My life is forever changing but I think I'm pretty positive because I am around people who are positive."

☆ "I feel that I'm becoming a wiser woman because I learn from my experiences and I know what to do and what to say when it happens again."

Ten Ways to Become a Powerful Woman

1 Educate yourself.
2 Find role models.
3 Speak your mind.
4 Believe in yourself.
5 Don't depend on a guy.
6 Don't judge people.
7 Get a job that you like and that teaches you something.
8 Surround yourself with positive energy.
9 Spend time with your family.
10 Communicate with, respect, and support other women.

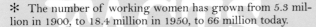

FACTS

✳ The number of working women has grown from 5.3 million in 1900, to 18.4 million in 1950, to 66 million today.

✳ Women made up 18% of the labor force in 1900 and 30% in 1950. They make up 47% of the labor force today.

✳ 99 out of every 100 women in the United States will work for pay at some point in their life.

Source: AFL-CIO

The Women's Cypher
by Jewnbug, 24

Girls, young ladies, women
comparing and contrasting
on positive notes
living by inspirational quotes.
coming together and rebuilding
foundations to overcome frustrations
with faith, not just hopes.
from all walks of life
living in nature's proverbs
hungering for human rights,
producing by planting seeds
to visualize and embrace
the connection we share
with water and sky
forming family ties.
revolution revitalizing times
acknowledging divine presence
in all living things
in harmony and rhyme.
creating and growing
respecting diverse expressions
encouraging explorations
to unite as
One Sisterhood Nation.

What woman do you admire?
How does she express her personal power?

☆ " My mom. She is the most noble person I know. She taught and raised us really good. How does it feel to have a mom like mine? I don't know. I've only had one mother and she's the person who I love most. What I admire is everything. There are so many things I love that not everything would fit on this paper no matter how small the words. What I admire the most is that she loves us no matter what."

☆ " One person that stands out for me is Frieda Kahlo. Her art—drawings and paintings—are so real. She is honest through her art and it seems to me that she didn't hesitate at all. She exposed every feeling. I like that a lot. It's like she didn't care what everybody thought of her. I really admire her a lot."

☆ " I'm proud of many women who are successful in their jobs and help people who are in trouble with their intelligence, kindness, and love."

☆ " My mom 'cause when she was a child she had a real tough mom and a swell dad. At 12 she lost her father, one of the toughest things she has ever had to go through. When she got married to my dad, my grandma got mad at her and wouldn't talk to her. It almost killed her. My dad worked in the U.S. trying to help my mom who was living alone in Mexico taking care of three kids. She was tough on us for awhile until we moved in with my dad. Then she saw that my dad was also tough on us and she realized she didn't want to be like her mother so she decided to change. She is there to listen to me and give me advice and of course gets mad when I do something wrong."

How will things be different for young women in the future?

☆ " Young women shouldn't be sexually harassed on the streets. They shouldn't be afraid to speak their minds. They shouldn't feel like the media—newspaper, music— defines who they are or gives them an image of what is beautiful."

☆ " I think young women will become stronger and more independent in the future because they will be given more resources and more encouragement to do so."

☆ " I think that women will have more opportunities to do things for themselves than ever. I think that one day we will have a female president. Also women will have more of a voice and representation in decisions that deal with our communities and government and how it's set up."

☆ " I think and I hope people treat young women the same as men in the future. And that young women can be strong and stand up for themselves."

"When I dare to be powerful—to use my strength in the service of my vision, then it becomes less and less important whether I am afraid."

Audre Lorde

FUTURE

Resources

Our Minds & Souls

Sexuality

National Gay and Lesbian Hotline 1-800-347-TEEN (6:30-9:00 PM every day)

Lavender Youth Recreation and Information Center (LYRIC) www.lyric.org
LYRIC Youth Talkline: 1-800-246-PRIDE (6:30-9:30 PM PST, every day)
For lesbian, gay, bisexual, transgender, queer, and questioning youth. Call this number to talk anonymously (in English or Spanish) to other youth about sexuality and gender issues.

PlanetOut www.planetout.com
Site for gay women and men providing articles and interviews on history, pride, entertainment, politics, and family.

Free Your Mind: The Book for Gay, Lesbian, and Bisexual Youth—and Their Allies. Ellen Bass and Kate Kaufman; Harper Collins (1996).

The Underground Guide to Teenage Sexuality. Michael J. Basso; Fairview Press, Minnesota (1997).

Emotional Health

Yellow Ribbon Suicide Prevention Program 1-800-784-2433 www.yellowribbon.org
Support and referrals to local services.

Teen Crisis Hotline 1-800-840-5704 (24-hour hotline)

Yellow Ribbon Grief Line 1-800-837-1818
For families and individuals who have lost someone close to them. Call this number 24 hours a day for someone to talk with and referrals to grief counseling.

Death and Dying Grief Support www.death-dying.com
Get resources for dealing with loss, a special section for teens, and message boards to read others' stories or share your own.

Our Bodies

Playing Sports

Women's Sports Foundation 1-800-227-3988 (Monday-Friday, 9 AM to 5 PM)
www.womenssportsfoundation.org
A member-based organization that provides scholarships and grants to young women athletes. Call to ask sports-related questions and to gain access to their information database.

Body Image and Eating Disorders

National Association of Anorexia Nervosa and Associated Disorders (ANAD)
1-847-831-3438 (Monday-Friday 9 AM to 5 PM Central Time) www.anad.org/info.htm

Eating Disorders Awareness and Prevention 1-800-931-2237 www.nationaleatingdisorders.org

Something Fishy Website on Eating Disorders www.something-fishy.org
Highly informative site that includes articles, resources, links to other sites, chat rooms, and an online newsletter.

Adios, Barbie: Young Women Write About Body Image and Identity. Ophira Edut, ed.; Seal Press Feminist Publications (March 1998).

FAT! SO? Because You Don't Have to Apologize for Your Size. Marilyn Wann; Ten Speed Press (January 1999). www.fatso.com

Drugs and Substance Abuse

Center for Substance Abuse Hotline 1-800-662-HELP (1-800-662-4357)
24-hour hotline for referrals to substance abuse treatment in your area.

National Council on Alcoholism and Drug Dependence 1-800-475-HOPE (1-800-475-4673)
www.ncadd.org
Education, information, and help for alcohol and drug addictions.

Alcoholics Anonymous www.aa.org
A good resource if you or a person close to you drinks too much.

DanceSafe www.dancesafe.org
Promoting health and safety within the rave and nightclub community.

From Chocolate to Morphine: Everything You Need to Know about Mind-Altering Drugs. Andrew Weil and Winifred Rosen; Houghton-Mifflin, New York (1998).

Tattooing and Body Art

Tattoo and Piercing Studio Directory www.tat2studios.com
Referrals to over 100 tattoo websites, artists' tattoo gallery, national and international studio directory.

ICS Directory on Bodyart www.cs.uu.nl/wais/html/na-dir/bodyart/.html
Answers to frequently asked questions (FAQ) about tattooing and piercing.

STIs, HIV and AIDS

National STD Hotline 1-800-227-8922 (24-hour hotline)

HIV/AIDS Teen Hotline 1-800-440-TEEN (Fridays and Saturdays, 6 PM to 12 AM EST)

I Wanna Know www.iwannaknow.org
Answers to teen questions about sexual health and STD prevention.

Sexually Transmitted Diseases: A Physician Tells You What You Need to Know. Lisa Marr; Johns Hopkins University Press, Baltimore (1998).

Birth Control and Pregnancy

Planned Parenthood http://www.plannedparenthood.org/teens/index.html
Puberty, abstinence, birth control, pregnancy, abortion, body image, and other health issues plus a clinic locator map.

Abortion

National Abortion Federation (NAF) 1-800-772-9100 (Monday–Friday, 9 AM to 7 PM EST) www.prochoice.org
Clear, balanced answers on abortion, your rights, and references to clinics.

Planned Parenthood 1-800-230-PLAN
Provides medical information and will direct you to your local clinic.

Adoption

AdoptioNetwork www.adoption.org
Fair, friendly adoption information.

Parenting

hipMama www.hipmama.com
An online magazine about the reality of being a young single mother.

National Fatherhood Initiative www.fatherhood.org
Info for young men who want to become responsible loving parents.

Sex

Planned Parenthood Federation of America's Teenwire www.teenwire.com
Sexuality and relationship info.

Sex, etc. www.sxetc.org
A website by and for teens about sex and sexuality.

Teen Advice Online www.teenadvice.org
Advice from other teens about dating, sex, relationships, family issues, and more.

Smart Sex. Jessica Vitkus, Marjorie Ingall, and Jessica Weeks; Pocket Books (March1998).

Our Relationships

Child Abuse and Domestic Violence

Child Help USA/ National Child Abuse Hotline 1-800-4-A-CHILD (1-800-422-4453)
Call for counseling or information about child abuse-related issues.

National Domestic Violence/Abuse Hotline 1-800-799-SAFE (1-800-799-7233)
Call this 24-hour hotline for information and referrals to local groups that can help you with domestic violence problems, including abusive girlfriends or boyfriends.

Domestic Violence and Incest Resource Centre www.dvirc.org.au/
Also check out their page called, "When love hurts: A guide for girls on abuse in relationships" at www.dvirc.org.au/whenlove/

In Love and In Danger: A Teen's Guide to Breaking Free of Abusive Relationships. Barrie Levy; Seal Press Feminist Publishers (February 1998). Also available in Spanish.

Our Rights

Rape

Rape, Abuse, and Incest National Network (RAINN) 1-800-656-HOPE (1-800-656-4673) www.rainn.org
Information, links, and community organizing.

Voices of Rape. Janet Bode; Franklin Watts Inc., New York (1998).
Written in a very youth-friendly style. Bode gives first-person accounts of rape victims to show psychological, physical, and legal aspects.

Running Away
California Youth Crisis Line 1-800-843-5200 (8 AM-midnight, Spanish and English)
www.ccyfc.org
> Provides confidential crisis counseling and shelter referrals for at risk homeless youth.

National Runaway Switchboard 1-800-621-4000 (24 hours)

Legal Services
American Civil Liberties Union www.aclu.org
> Information on students' rights, immigrants' rights, racial equality, and more.

American Civil Liberties Union Handbooks for Young Americans: The Rights of Women and Girls.
Kary Moss and Norman Dorsen; Puffin (1998).

American Civil Liberties Union Handbooks for Young Americans: The Rights of Racial Minorities.
John A. Powell, Laughlin McDonald, and Norman Dorsen; Puffin (March 1998).

What Are My Rights?: 95 Questions and Answers About Teens and the Law. Thomas A. Jacobs,
J.D.; Free Spirit (October 1997).

Immigration
Immigration and Naturalization Services (INS) 1-800-870-3676
> Forms request hotline. Spanish and English.

Our Futures

Strong Young Women
Cybergrrl www.cybergrrl.com
> Along with a chat room, articles by young women on technology, sports, travel, music,
books, health, writing, and much more.

Career and Job Search
The Personality Page www.personalitypage.com
> Myers-Briggs questionnaire that can be applied to career, relationships, and personal growth.

Girls Unlimited: Dream Big, Prepare Well www.girlsunlimited.com
> Lets girls explore different career possibilities.

Choosing a College
All About College www.allaboutcollege.com
> Links to colleges and universities worldwide.

Peterson's College Quest www.petersons.com/ugchannel/
> Comparisons of colleges and universities: courses of study, financial aid, student mix, and more.

College Testing
Fair Test: SAT/ACT Optional Schools www.fairtest.org/optional.htm
> State-by-state and alphabetical listings of schools and facts about standardized testing biases.

Educational Testing Service Network www.ets.org
> Admissions testing prep, resources, and test dates and locations.

College Financial Aid
Federal Student Aid Information Center 1-800-4-FED-AID (1-800-433-3243)

FinAid www.finaid.org
> The smart guide to student financial aid: applications, loans, scholarships, military aid, and more.

U.S. Dept. of Education Student Guide to Financial Aid
> http://studentaid.ed.gov/students/publications/student_guide/index.html

A Little Bit of Everything

Teen Voices Online www.teenvoices.com
> National magazine for, by, and about young women.

TeensHealth www.teenshealth.org/index.html
> Links to articles on all kinds of health topics for teens.

A Young Woman's Survival Guide. Health Initiatives for Youth, San Francisco (1998).
> Available at www.hify.org/survival_guide.htm

Changing Bodies, Changing Lives. Ruth Bell with members of the Teen Book Project; Times Books,
New York (1998).

Our Bodies, Ourselves for the New Century: A Book by and for Women. Boston Women's Health
Book Collective; Touchstone Press, New York (1998).

Women's Bodies, Women's Wisdom. Christiane Northrup, M.D.; Bantam Doubleday Dell Publishers
(March 1998) (Trade Paperback).

Sources

Mind/Soul

Abner, Allison and Linda Villarosa. *Finding Our Way: The Teen Girl's Survival Guide*. New York: HarperPerennial, 1996.

Bethards, Betty and Jaclyn Catalfo. *The Way of the Mystic: Seven Steps to Developing Your Intuitive Powers*. London: HarperCollins UK, 1995.

DeBord, Karen, "Challenges & Choices: Emotional Well-Being—Women's Self-Esteem," *Human Environmental Sciences* publication (University of Missouri-Columbia) GH6652 (1997).

Digiulio, Robert and Rachel Kranz. *Straight Talk About Death and Dying*. New York: Facts on File, Inc., 1995.

Lorde, Audre. *Sister Outsider*. Berkeley, CA: Crossing Press, 1984.

Reder, Alan, Phil Catalfo, and Stephanie Renfrow Hamilton. *The Whole Parenting Guide: Strategies, Resources, and Inspiring Stories for Holistic Parenting and Family Living*. New York: Broadway Books, 1999.

Wolf, Anthony E. *Get Out of My Life, but First Could You Drive Me & Cheryl to the Mall: A Parent's Guide to the New Teenager*. New York: Farrar, Strauss & Giroux, 1992.

American Association of Suicidology (n.d.) Retrieved 2000, from www.suicidology.org/

Lavender Youth Recreation and Information Center (LYRIC) (n.d.) Retrieved 2000, from www.lyric.org/

Parents, Families and Friends of Lesbians and Gays (PFLAG) (n.d.) Retrieved 2000, from www.pflag.org/

Bodies

Aguirre, Yesenia, ed. *A Young Woman's Survival Guide*. San Francisco: Health Initiatives for Youth, 1998.

A Report of the Surgeon General. *Physical Activity and Health At-A-Glance*, 1996.

Basso, Michael J. *The Underground Guide to Teenage Sexuality: An Essential Handbook for Today's Teens and Parents*. Minneapolis: Fairview Press, 1997.

The Boston Women's Health Book Collective. *The New Our Bodies, Ourselves: A Book by and for Women*. New York: Touchstone Press, 1992.

Barbach, Lonnie. *For Yourself: The Fulfillment of Female Sexuality*. New York: Doubleday, 1976.

Beyer, Kay. *Coping with Teen Parenting*. New York: Rosen Publishing Group, 1995.

Burns, A. August, Sandy Niemann, and Elena Metcalf. *Where Women Have No Doctor: A Health Guide for Women*. Berkeley: Hesperian Foundation, 1997.

Chabon, Brenda and Donna Futterman, "Adolescents and HIV," *AIDS Clinical Care*, vol. 11, no. 2 (February 1999).

Inaba, Darryl, William E. Cohen, and Michael E. Holstein. *Uppers, Downers, All Arounders: Physical and Mental Effects of Psychoactice Drugs*. Ashland, OR: CNS Publications, 1993.

Julien, Robert M. *A Primer of Drug Action: A Concise, Non-Technical Guide to the Actions, Uses, and Side Effects of Psychoactive Drugs*. New York: W.H. Freeman & Co., 1985.

Montreal Health Press. *The STD Handbook*. Montreal: Montreal Health Press, 1999.

Reder, Alan, Phil Catalfo, and Stephanie Renfrow Hamilton. *The Whole Parenting Guide: Strategies, Resources, and Inspiring Stories for Holistic Parenting and Family Living*. New York: Broadway Books, 1999.

Stewart, Felicia Hance. *My Body, My Health: The Concerned Woman's Book of Gynecology*. New York: Bantam Books, 1981.

Stewart, Gail B. *Teen Mothers*. San Diego: Lucent Books, 1996.

Werner, David, Carol Thuman, and Jane Maxwell. *Where There Is No Doctor: A Village Health Care Handbook*. Berkeley: Hesperian Foundation, 1999.

Planned Parenthood Federation of America (n.d.) Retrieved 2000 from www.plannedparenthood.org/bc/

Relationships

Resnick, Stella. *The Pleasure Zone: Why We Resist Good Feelings and How to Let Go and Be Happy*. Berkeley: Conari Press, 1997.

Domestic Violence & Incest Resource Centre (n.d.) Retrieved 2000 from www.dvirc.org.au

Rights

Legal Services for Children, Inc. *Emancipation Guide: Questions and Answers about Emancipation for Teenagers*. San Francisco: Legal Services for Children, Inc., 1998.

Student Leaders Against Sexual Harassment. *Report on Sexual Harassment*. San Francisco: Student Leaders Against Sexual Harassment (S.L.A.S.H.), 1999.

Democratic Leadership Committees (n.d.) *Before Title IX*. Retrieved May 19, 2000 from www.senate.gov/~dpc/events/970618/facts.html

Girls Incorporated. *Girls' Bill of Rights*. (n.d.) Retrieved 2000 from www.girlsinc.com/ic/content/GirlsBillofRights.pdf

National Runaway Switchboard (n.d.) *A Profile of Runaway and Homeless Youth Nationwide*. Retrieved June 25, 2000 from www.nrscrisiline.org/stats.htm

The Rape, Abuse & Incest National Network (n.d.) *RAINN Statistics*. Retrieved March 20, 2000 from www.rainn.org/

U.S. Department of Education (1997). *Title IX: 25 Years of Progress*. Retreived June 25, 2000 from www.ed.gov/pubs/TitleIX/part2.html

U.S. Department of Justice, Office of Justice Programs (1995) *Violence Against Women: Estimates from the Redesigned Survey*. Retrieved March 19, 2000 from www.ojp.usdoj.gov/bjs/pub/ascii/femvied.txt

Futures

FairTest. *FairTest Fact Sheet: The Sat.* (n.d.) Retrieved May 30, 2000 from www.fairtest.org/facts/satfact/htm

Women's Financial Network (n.d.) Retrieved 2000 from www.wfn.com/

Acknowledgments

We couldn't have done this book without you. You are our volunteers, advisors, professional experts, friends, supporters, readers, researchers, young women, survey participants, poets, models, artists, and sister community organizations. Thank you for all the ways you made this project possible and meaningful! (Our apologies for omissions and misspellings.)

To all of the organizations and young women in San Francisco, Los Angeles, New York, and other cities who participated in the survey and focus groups that helped determine which issues were addressed in this book:
In San Francisco, Bayview Hunters Point Department of Youth Services, Center City Hospitality House, The Center for Young Women's Development, Chinatown Youth Center, Cole Street Youth Clinic, Galileo High School, Girls After School Academy (GASA), Health Initiatives for Youth (HIFY), Hilltop High School, Lavender Youth Recreation and Information Center (LYRIC), New Generation Health Center, Precita Valley Community Center, and San Francisco Women Against Rape (SFWAR); in Oakland, American Indian Child Resource Center (AICRC) and Women's Economic Agenda Project (WEAP); in Los Angeles, Bienestar Human Services, Reach L.A., and Y.W.C.A.; and in other cities, Minneapolis Coalition Against Sexual Assault Resource Services and Planned Parenthood in the Bronx.

To the professionals and experts who provided information on issues and know-how on production:
Tsan Abrahamson, Kim Arroyo, Nia Blackston, Patti Breitman, Lori Dobeus, Dewitt Durham, Sharon Emery, Allen Fitzpatrick, Bill Hackethal, Lynne Henderson, Caroline Herter, Adela Lam, Meredith Larson, Nancy Lewis, Gary McDonald, Connie Mendez, Dave Paisley, Eumeka Pargo, Meg Scott, Anne Tamar-Matis, and Ann Tardy.

To our expert readers who made thoughtful comments and suggestions:
Lamia Chlala, Sarah Church, Marta Cruz, Shalini Eddens, Jewnbug, Mona Jhawar, Erika Lindsey, Lisa Margonelli, Kelly O'Neill, Estelle Rubenstein, Becca Schwartz, Meg Scott, Irela Valderrama, and Jill Weinberg.

To our community of advisors and friends who generously shared their vision, wisdom, experiences, support, and resources along the way:
Theresa Alvarez, Deborah Alvarez-Rodriguez, Hilary Beech, Melissa Bradley, Jennifer Elias, Pat Forman, Elizabeth Gettelman, Seth Godin, Kaz Hashimoto, Mary Isham and Sandra Martinez, Michael Korson, Meredith Maran, Arminda Montoya, Shireen Lee, Lawrence Levy, Fran Ravel, Liz Schaffer, Salila Shen; Britta Beenhakker, Cole Street Youth Clinic; Maria Cora, Special Programs for Youth; Amanda Goldberg, Planned Parenthood; Priya Jaganathan, Glide Memorial Church; Anna Landau, Link Exchange; Sara Littlecrow-Russel, National Young Women's Day of Action; Cindy Moon, NAWHO; Monique Noveros, GASA; Melina O'Grady, Bay Area Teen Voices; Elizabeth O'Malley, New Generation Health Center; Lateefah Simon, Center for Young Women's Development; Julie Sparling, CELL Space; Brianna Visser, Precita Valley Community Center; Krishanti Dharmaraj and Kate Washburn, WILD; Aryn Faur and Jane Maxwell, Hesperian Foundation; Vivien Labaton and Amy Richards, Third Wave Foundation; Jennifer Melsher and Kar Yin Tham, CUAV; Kelly O'Neill and Rachel Pfeffer, The Young Women's Work Project; Kim Compoc, Lissette Flores, and Twilight Greenaway, HIFY; and Scott Lekovish, David Long, and Christian Semmel, V.2 Consulting.

To our dedicated volunteer interns:
The dynamic duo of Arlen Grad and Cheryl Labe; Thelmisha Vincent, and Katherine Weaver.

Thank You

To the Young Women's Outreach Team:
Veronica Castro, Lourdes Llanes, Kevina Mitchell, and Treja Stutts.

To the young women and men who let us photograph them and allowed us to include their ideas, quotes, interviews, stories, and poetry:
Crystal Anthony, Brian Babcock, Kevin Briancesco, Crystal Burkett, Jose Carrasco, Danielle Edwards, Veronica Greenhouse, Antonia Gristi, Trayce Groves, Jewnbug, Brenda Lawrence, Gabrielle Magpiong, Sara Melia, Thomisla Peen, Sandra Silva, Danny Tamayo, Katherine Tapia, Keilani K. Tearpa, Erica Trujillo, Gonzalo Valdivia, Maria Del Carmen Villalobos, Margarita Watkins, Willdora, and Wendy Wong.

To the dedicated production team that helped turn this project into a real book:
Christina Boufis, Ken DellaPenta, Stephanie Hamilton, Deb Levine, Melissa Lucas, Lisa Margonelli, Diana Reiss-Koncar, Mercedes Romero, and Gayle Steinbeigle.

To past GirlSource staff for their vision and very hard work on this project:
Jodi Perelman and Sophy Shihua Wong.

To our family and board of directors (past and present):
Linda Adler, Theresa Alvarez, Aisha Bilal, Shannon Buscho, Ani Chamichian, Ana Chavez, Molly Coye, Brenda Dyer, Pat Forman, Judy Frabotta, Lea Gamble, Elizabeth Givens, Rachael Grossman, Kimberly Guilfoyle-Newsom, Caroline Herter, Diana Kapp, Priya Mathur, Krystal Maxwell, Janis Medina, Bessie Natareno, Willa Seldon, Maryann Simpson, Lina Shatara, Ann Tardy, Glady Thacher, and Dania Wasongarz.

And also to:
The Women's Foundation for incubating us as our fiscal sponsor for the first year; Carolina Gonzalez-Villar, Community Health Educator at Planned Parenthood Golden Gate and Jon Knowles, Director of Public Information at Planned Parenthood Federation of America; Kirsty Melville and Metha Klock at Ten Speed Press.

Credits

Lynn Gordon, GirlSource Founding Director

GirlSource Staff
Anne Moses, Executive Director
Sarah Benjamin, Sara Brissenden-Smith, Laura Feinstein, Abigail Kramer, Holly Million, Erika Padilla-Morales, Kaila Price, Lisa Raymond, Sonia Swindell

Original Production Team
Production Management: Lynn Gordon
Program Director: Youmna Chlala
Outreach Coordinator: Myrna Valderrama
Graphic Design: Gayle Steinbeigle, Protopod Design
Photography: Mercedes Romero
Writing: Stephanie Renfrow Hamilton, Diana Reiss-Koncar, Christina Boufis
Editing: Deb Levine, Lisa Margonelli
Copy Editing: Melissa Lucas

Revised Edition Production Team
Produced by Herter Studio LLC
Project Management: Debbie Berne
Cover and title page design: Nina J. Miller, Nina Miller Design
Cover photograph: Gabriella Hasbun
Copyediting: Simone Solondz

Photography
Mercedes Romero – pp. 10, 16, 18, 19, 22, 23, 25, 30, 32, 35, 41, 43, 51, 52, 55, 56, 58, 59, 63, 66, 68, 71, 73
Gabriella Hasbun – p. 2
Mieka Valdez – p. 21
Sierra Murphree – p. 15

Illustration
Lina Shatara – pp. 5, 6, 11, 26, 27, 30, 31, 63, 77, 87
Diana Valdivia – pp. 65, 71, 78, 81, 84, 85, 86
Diana Reiss-Koncar – pp. 35, 37
Wanda Chan – pp. 53, 88
Please note that additional doodles throughout the book are the creation of different young women.

Index

Index

A Kirsty Melville Book

1☉

Ten Speed Press
P.O. Box 7123
Berkeley, CA 94707
www.tenspeed.com

GirlSource, Inc.
1550 Bryant Street, Suite 675
San Francisco, CA 94103
415-252-8880
book@girlsource.org
www.girlsource.org

GirlSource, Inc. is a 501(c)(3) nonprofit organization supported by individuals, corporations, and foundation and government grants. Your support makes projects like this possible! Learn more about our organization, programs, and this book at www.girlsource.org.

We're interested in learning how you used this book and what you found useful. Write to us!

ISBN 1-58008-555-5

Library of Congress Cataloging-in-Publication Data
on file with publisher.

Printed in China
First printing: August 2003

1 2 3 4 5 6 7 8 9 10 — 05 04 03 02 01

0673